CW00509237

THE MARRANO SPECTER

The Marrano Specter

DERRIDA AND HISPANISM

ERIN GRAFF ZIVIN

Editor

FORDHAM UNIVERSITY PRESS

New York 2018

Copyright © 2018 Fordham University Press

All rights reserved. No part of this publication may be
reproduced, stored in a retrieval system, or transmitted in
any form or by any means—electronic, mechanical,
photocopy, recording, or any other—except for brief
quotations in printed reviews, without the prior permission
of the publisher.

Fordham University Press has no responsibility for the
persistence or accuracy of URLs for external or third-party
Internet websites referred to in this publication and does not
guarantee that any content on such websites is, or will
remain, accurate or appropriate.

Fordham University Press also publishes its books in a
variety of electronic formats. Some content that appears in
print may not be available in electronic books.

Visit us online at www.fordhampress.com.

Library of Congress Cataloging-in-Publication Data
available online at https://catalog.loc.gov.

Printed and bound in Great Britain by
Marston Book Services Limited, Oxfordshire

20 19 18   5 4 3 2 1
First edition

CONTENTS

Peggy Kamuf

Some of the most vibrant Hispanists working in the United States today are the authors of the essays in this volume, *The Marrano Specter: Derrida and Hispanism*, which emerged from the 2014 conference on the topic. The essayists agreed to reflect on the figure of the marrano as a way into questions about their field from the angles of the sort of "theory" Hispanism has long reproved and resisted, for the marrano also plays a significant role in the late work of Jacques Derrida, recurring there with some frequency. By pairing the field's name with Derrida's, the title of the present volume opens the space of an encounter into which the essays collected here advance at their different rhythms.

The marrano, as traced by Derrida over the last dozen years of his life's work, is taken on there at multiple levels, beginning perhaps with the level of personal identification out of which unfold various figures of universalization. The identification arises out of the childhood experience among the Jews of Algiers who called circumcision "baptism" and Bar Mitzvah "communion," through a strange kind of assimilation to or compromise with the dominant Christian culture in which Judaism survives in remnants. In *Circumfession* (1991), Derrida confesses or feigns to confess: "I am a sort of marrano of French Catholic culture . . . one of those marranos who no longer say they are Jews even in the secret of their own hearts, not so as to be authenticated as marranos on both sides of the public frontier, but because they doubt everything, never go to confession or give up enlightenment" (170–71).

But from there the figure of the marrano is carried by a force of universalization to which Derrida gives explicit voice. In *Aporias* (1992) marrano comes to name the universal condition of an impossible relation to death as to a secret. "Let us figuratively call marrano anyone who remains faithful to a secret that he has not chosen, in the very place where he lives, in the home of the inhabitant or of the occupant, in the home of the first or of the second *arrivant*, in the very place where he sojourns without saying no but without identifying himself as belonging to" (81). Elsewhere, in "Abraham, the Other" (2003), Derrida patiently works out this transposition of singular experience into universal description. At one point, addressing himself in the figure of the marrano, he reads off its paradoxical law: "The less you show yourself as jewish, the more and better jew you will be. The more radically you break with a certain dogmatism of the place and the bond (communal, national, religious, of the state), the more you will be faithful to the hyperbolic, excessive demand, to the *hubris*, perhaps, of a universal and disproportionate responsibility toward the singularity of every other" (13). The marrano axiomatic of more-than equals less-than or other-than is associated by Derrida with his mistrust of frontiers and oppositional distinctions, impelling him, as he writes, "to elaborate a deconstruction as well as an ethics of decision or of responsibility exposed to the endurance of the undecidable" (17). Marrano thus names a hyperbolic, universal responsibility, a fidelity that breaks with every community, a secret destiny that sojourns without belonging, a dissociation that inhabits the social bond.

This latter essay, "Abraham, the Other," is in part a reading of a Kafka parable titled simply "Abraham." There Kafka repeatedly invokes "another Abraham," "other Abrahams," for example, one who could not get away from the house however much he was willing to answer the call to sacrifice. Or "take another Abraham," says Kafka, who likewise was ready to do the right thing, but he cannot believe that he was the Abraham addressed by the call. He fears being foolish and that "the world would laugh itself to death at the sight of him." Just imagine if the worst student in the class thinks his name has been called to receive a prize meant for the best student: "He came forward from his dirty desk in the last row because he had made a mistake of hearing and the whole class burst out laughing." In the midst of all these misprisions and malentendus, this other Abraham at one point fears that, if he answers the call, he will turn into someone else, and not just anyone else: "He is afraid that after starting out as Abraham with his son he would change on the way into Don Quixote."

Don Quixote? Even though, in his selective reading of the parable, Derrida does not wonder about this allusion to one of the foundational works of Hispanism, others now come forward here to pursue the reflection in the shadow of Cervantes, but also of Bolaño, Borges, Cortázar. It is a reflection on marranismo as it arises out of the language that first lent cover in that name to the refractory subjects who all the same respond, "Yes, here I am," like the other Abraham. Marrano was meant to have the force of insult, injury, *injure* in French, at once insult and injury. It was meant to be a wounding word. Swine. Dirty. Outcast. But at the same time marrano deflects, absorbs, or shelters in secret the other name. It keeps the one who keeps the secret. One is "entrusted for safekeeping, entrusted to a silence that keeps and guards so long as one keeps and guards it" ("Abraham, the Other," 6).

About a quarter century ago, in 1992, was the five-hundredth anniversary of the expulsion of the Jews from Spain. It was also, of course, the anniversary of the year Columbus gave the Old World a foothold in the New and took a first step toward the vast Spanish empire to come in the Americas. And in the same year, with the fall of Granada, Arabs were driven out of a newly unified and uniformly Catholic Spain. *Annus mirabilis, annus horribilis.* If we call Hispanists those who inherit and respond to this immense legacy in trust for the rest of us, then this volume is testimony to a trust well placed.

Los Angeles
January 2016

WORKS CITED

Jacques Derrida, "Abraham, the Other." 2003. In *Judeities: Questions for Jacques Derrida*, edited by Bettina Bergo, Joseph Cohen, and Raphael Zagury-Orly, 1–35. New York: Fordham University Press, 2007.

———. *Aporias.* 1992. Stanford: Stanford University Press, 1993.

———. *Circumfession.* 1991. In *Jacques Derrida*, translated by Geoffrey Bennington, 3–315. Chicago: University of Chicago Press, 1993.

THE MARRANO SPECTER

Introduction: Derrida's Marranismo

Erin Graff Zivin

> The fact that I fell in love with this word [*marrane*] that
> has become a kind of obsession, figuring in most of my
> recent works, is because it refers to supposed Judeo-Spanish
> origins but also because it evokes a culture of secrecy.
>
> —JACQUES DERRIDA, *D'ailleurs, Derrida*

"Why are Latin Americanists so interested in specters?" Peggy Kamuf asked me several years ago.[1] It's true: For the past twenty years, Latin Americanists, and to a different degree and in different ways Hispanists who focus on the Iberian peninsula, have taken up ghosts, *revenants*, *hantologie*, specters, and *Specters of Marx* with particular focus. How have Latin Americanists, or Hispanists, read Derrida? *Which* Derrida have they read and *how*? What are the motifs that draw us? What are the questions that compel us, that beckon to us? We can venture a guess, a hypothesis (or two or three). We might guess that more, or quite different sorts of, ghosts haunt the Hispanic world, or the worlds of Hispanism, than haunt even such notoriously ghosted academic fields as the novel (Ian Watt's account is awash with colonial revenants and goblins), Victorian and Romantic studies (Gothic madwomen in the attic with Caribbean connections), political economy, and European studies (communism's famous specter), and so on. Or we might guess that *Specters of Marx*, in which Derrida first developed the notion of hauntology, poses a particular demand to scholars of the Hispanophone world. We can say that many who have taken up the work of Jacques Derrida from the politically charged fields of Hispanism and Latin

Americanism find the ethical or political inflection in Derrida's later writings alluring. We might even hypothesize, somewhat cynically, that the question of justice as Derrida poses it enables us to justify what we do in the academy. Perhaps the uneven modernization of Latin America and its effects on the cultural field translate into a particular affinity with the idea of untimeliness, of time being out of joint, that rings in Hamlet's words through Derrida's book: "The time is out of joint; O cursed spite, / That ever I was born to set it right!" (1.5.211–12).

But why Derrida *today*? Have Latin Americanists once again arrived late at the banquet of European civilization, as Alfonso Reyes proclaimed in 1936? Is it untimely, intempestive, to speak of Derrida now, decades after, we are told, deconstruction and "theory" more broadly have receded from the academic limelight? Finally, has a "belated" focus on the "late" Derrida kept us from reading other, earlier Derrida texts, kept us from understanding the complex and unexpected ways in which Derrida's work might pertain to Latin Americanism and Hispanism?

We could pose these questions somewhat differently: What kinds of specters haunt Hispanism? And could we not flip the accusation of belatedness and suggest that Hispanism's engagement with Derrida can allow aspects of his work unmarked by other disciplines and approaches to come into relief, now more than before, and with important consequences for how Derrida is to be read even beyond the bounds of Hispanism and Latin Americanism? These concerns motivate the present volume, which considers not only how disciplines are formed, or what they expel, or necessarily exclude in order to cement their boundaries and practices (and which will return in ghostly form), but also, more optimistically, the question of what happens, how we can attend to, guard, even care for those spectral exclusions if we are to consider them internal, constitutive, to the discipline. A first step: We can think about something as inwardly regarding as an academic discipline, or as disciplinarity in general, as an ethicopolitical field, or a field constituted about a set of conceptions of ethics and politics. When it comes to Hispanism, just what these conceptions are and thus what an ethicopolitical Hispanism, or an ethics or politics of Hispanism, might look like, is not at all clear. These essays, individually and together, don't seek in Derrida's work a tool or a method. Each in a different way puts into question the technical and disciplinary reconstruction of Derrida's work, which is the pendant to the pervasive, journalistic mischaracterization of deconstruction in the UK and the United States over the past decades.

A number of the contributors turn to a figure from the history of the Hispanic world for a description of, even a name for, this ethicopolitical kernel that organizes the disciplines of Latin Americanism and Hispanic studies—a figure of an identity expelled and internalized, rejected, translated and converted, subject to violence, forgotten.[2] A figure of exile and return, or of a double exclusion, as José Luis Villacañas has argued. The marrano is a figure in two moments of a broader political operation: the simultaneous expulsion and conversion of the Jews, two faces of the same project to consolidate a reunified, Christianized Spain. Marranismo, inasmuch as it is a figure of exclusion-introjection, then, comes to signify that which continues to haunt Hispanism, a fold or a fault line within Hispanism.

Of course, we could also ask the inverse question: How can we identify a marrano inflection in Derrida's work? Yes, Derrida's thinking has had a unique impact on Hispanism, distinct from its influence on other fields of study, but what strange effects of the Hispanic world are traceable in Derrida's writing? As we know from *Circumfession* (1991), *Aporias* (1992), "History of the Lie: Prolegomena" (1993), *Archive Fever* (1995), Safaa Fathy's documentary *D'ailleurs, Derrida* (1999), and Peggy Kamuf's foreword to this volume, the question of the *marrane* obsessed Derrida, not only because it provided him with a lexicon with which to complicate or reject Jewish identitarianism but also, perhaps more significantly, because it has stood alongside, inflected, and supplemented metonymically his preoccupation with secrecy and revelation, ethics and politics. "Naturally secrecy has always concerned me greatly, independently of my Jewish question," Derrida remarks in *D'ailleurs, Derrida*.

> It has concerned me not only in relation to the unconscious, to the political dimension of secrecy, secrecy being that which resists politics, that which resists politicization, citizenship, transparency, phenomenality. Wherever we seek to destroy secrecy or keeping secrets, there is a threat of totalitarianism. Totalitarianism is a crusher of secrecy: you will admit, you will confess, you will say what you really think. So the secret mission, the discreet mission of the Marrano is to teach the secret that secrets should be kept, should be respected. Secrecy should be held in respect. What is an absolute secret? I was obsessed with this question quite as much as that of my supposed Judeo-Spanish origins. These obsessions met in the figure of the Marrano. I gradually began to identify with someone who carries a secret that is bigger than himself and to which he does not have access. As if I were a Marrano's Marrano . . . a

lay Marrano, a Marrano who has lost the Jewish and Spanish origins of his Marranism, a kind of universal Marrano.

Thus the marrano enters Derrida's work to name an anti-identitarian category with which he can, paradoxically, express a certain identification: In *Archive Fever*, Derrida refers to "the Marranos, with whom I have always secretly identified (but don't tell anyone)" (46), a gesture that a number of scholars have taken up in recent years.

In her 2014 book *Jewish Cryptotheologies of Late Modernity: Philosophical Marranos*, Agata Bielik-Robson employs the term "philosophical Marranism" in order to refer to philosophers who, like Derrida, "will never break through the Joycean 'Jew-Greek, Greek-Jew' confusion, but nonetheless will try to turn it into his advantage. That is, to marry the speech of strangers and let the Hebrew talk through it: to do counter-philosophy with the help of philosophy" (4). Elsewhere, Bielik-Robson proposes the idea of a "marrano strategy" as an analogy between marranismo as religious practice and "the philosophical intervention of modern Jewish thinkers who spoke the seemingly universal idiom of Western philosophy but, at the same time, impregnated it 'secretly' with motives deriving from their 'particular' background."[3]

Although Bielik-Robson is interested first and foremost in marranismo as philosophical *strategy*, Graff Zivin, Hammerschlag, Kleinberg, and Norton underscore the way in which the figure of the marrano shakes and solicits the "Jew" as signifier in Derrida's oeuvre. Following the philosopher Ricardo Forster's claim that the marrano is the alter ego of the modern, autonomous, subject, whose fractured, failed wholeness exposes the impossibility of the modern subject, Graff Zivin draws on Derrida's marrano-as-metonym to expose the aporetic, impossible nature of subjectivity in the context of the Inquisition, as well as contemporary Inquisition narratives (2012).[4] In his essay "Not Yet Marrano: Levinas, Derrida, and the Ontology of Being Jewish," Ethan Kleinberg has underscored the nonexemplary exemplarity of the marrano in Derrida: "The Marrano is the exemplary 'crypto-X in general' but breaks down the logic of essentialism, of 'mineness,' authenticity, and exemplarity. . . . Indeed, at the moment one 'discovers' that one is a Marrano, the secret is revealed and thus one is a Marrano no longer" (55). In a similar vein, Sarah Hammerschlag argues that Derrida introduces the "as if" in relation to his Jewishness, or to Jewishness more broadly, through the figure of the marrano. Rather than guarding a hidden (but positive) Jewish essence, the marrano, for Derrida, "is the one who cannot claim Jewishness as his own. For to be a Marrano is to guard

Jewishness as an absolute secret, disruptive of all mineness [*Jemeinigkeit*], such that to know one's self as a Marrano is no longer to be one" (61).[5]

In addition to unsettling and displacing any fixed, proper sense of Jewishness (or identity in general), the figure of the marrano enters Derrida's work to signal a limit to absolute hegemony and state sovereignty: that which would resist or evade the play of hiding and revelation proper to classical notions of secrecy and therefore mark a limit to, say, inquisitional politics, to a form of politics that demands confessions, in which "everything must be made to appear in the transparency of the public space and its illumination . . . an absolute hegemony of political reason, a limitless extension of the region of the political" ("HL," 63).[6] Derrida loosens the tie to the specific history of crypto-Judaism and fashions a universal marrano—"the metonymic and generalized figure of the Marrano"—which he links to "the right to secrecy as right to resistance against and beyond the order of the political" (ibid., 64). The marrano, here, joins and reconfigures a familiar chain of signifiers in his work—*différance*, center, supplement, specter, *à-venir*, translation, trace—supplementing and unsettling them and, in turn, supplemented and unsettled by the others, opening a promising horizon for debates over the rapport between literature, ethics, and politics.

The question then becomes, for the contributors to this volume, not merely where and when Derrida has appeared, given lectures, been translated in, or been read by the Spanish-speaking world—a history that has been documented by Nelly Richard, Luis Ferrero Carracedo, Cristina de Peretti, and Delmiro Rocha[7]—but how to track and how to address the double movement of the Derridean trace in the world(s) of Hispanism and the Hispanist trace in Derrida's thought. This double movement reveals that what at first appear to be "local" concerns of Hispanists and Latin Americanists are in fact vital issues at the heart of Derrida's larger reception. Marrano thinking, for many of the contributors to this volume, comes to signify the very work of deconstruction. Against the reductive and reactionary misreadings of deconstruction's detractors, against the policing of deconstruction's borders by the faithful guardians of Derrida's legacy, marranismo becomes a provocative and promising trope: a model for thinking, in an age in which thinking seems to take place "only on the rarest of occasions."[8]

The essays in this volume, as well as the foreword by Peggy Kamuf and the afterword by Geoffrey Bennington, cut across this double fold— the marrano inflection within the work of Jacques Derrida's work and the Derridean or deconstructive inflection within Hispanism and Latin Americanism—by tackling some of the most urgent questions in university and intellectual life today. The body of the book is divided into three thematic parts. In the first part, "Marrano Indisciplinarity," Jacques Lezra, David Kelman, and Jaime Hanneken mine distinct conceptualizations of universalisms and universities through the analysis of three problems in Derrida's work: disciplinarity, monolingualism of the other, and what Derrida calls *mondialatinization*, making a case for rereading these Derridean concepts through a Hispanist, Latin Americanist, or marrano lens. In the opening essay, "Cervantes on 'Derrida': Hispanism in the Open," Jacques Lezra reads Cervantes's *novela ejemplar* "El licenciado Vidriera" as an allegory of disciplinarity and disciplinarization, arguing first that a lack of object fuels the political logic of empire (in Cervantes's time, the expanding Hapsburg empire; more recently, the melancholic loss of empire, in 1898, that helps shape contemporary Hispanism), and that, correspondingly, it is a lack of disciplinary object that ends up constituting disciplines, or the desire for disciplinarity. This lack, for Hispanism, bears the name marrano, so that just as the marrano stands as the condition of possibility and impossibility of Spanish imperialism, so too could it stand at the heart of Hispanism as its "secret and defective center." David Kelman, too, is interested in such internal *différance*, although in the field of comparative literature. Inspired by Derrida's idea of the "monolingualism of the other," Kelman asks what kind of comparatism could take place within rather than between languages or national literary traditions, a comparatism "in secret," a crypto-tradition that haunts every tradition. He calls such an intellectual practice "spectral comparison," a mode of reading that would attend to barely perceptible kernels of resistance at work in individual literary works as well as the "traditions" to which they are thought to belong. In "On Mondialatinization, or, Saving the Name of the Latin," Jaime Hanneken pursues the concept of mondialatinization, engaging with Derrida's attempt to deconstruct specifically Latin forms of global power while, counterintuitively, "saving" the name of the Latin. Hanneken asks what would be undeconstructible in Latin Americanism, how we could take apart the identitarianism that has structured the discipline without sacrificing the singularity that stands as its messianic possibility for change.

In the second part of this volume, "Form and Secrecy," Brett Levinson and Patrick Dove turn, or return, to form as a vital question not only for deconstruction but also, when read through the lens of marranismo, as a concept that bears a particular relation to secrecy. In his essay "The Jew or Patriarchy (or Worse)" Brett Levinson evaluates the status and function of the signifier "marrano" in Derrida, who places the figure alongside "all the other figures that he casts as irreducible to the signifier: pharmakon, writing, différance, *revenant*, specter, rogue, trace, gap, aporia, and many others." Just as the "Jew" in Derrida accompanies, supplements, and displaces other signifiers so that the signifier "Jew" is rescued from being a transcendental signifier, so too does the marrano displace the displaced signifier "Jew." The marrano thus becomes not a marker of a particular identity or a specific difference, but a marker of the play of differences that deconstruction puts into motion. Patrick Dove, in "Two Sides of the Same Coin? Form, Matter, and Secrecy in Derrida, de Man, and Borges," focuses on the relation between marranismo and secrecy, taking as his point of departure the marrano motif in the so-called late Derrida. He calls this periodization into question, suggesting that the designation of an "early" and "late" Derrida (the latter of which is thought to be more concerned with ethical and political questions) functions to distinguish Derrida from Paul de Man in an attempt to exonerate deconstruction after the de Man affair, when Paul de Man's early wartime journalism supporting the European fascist cultural program was revealed. Such a differentiation eclipses vital philosophical and linguistic problems treated in Derrida's and de Man's work that, when closely examined—here, with and through the work of Jorge Luis Borges—allow us to consider the ethical and political implications of form and secrecy.

In the volume's final part, "Between Nonethics and Infrapolitics," Gareth Williams, Alberto Moreiras, and Erin Graff Zivin press one specific aspect of marrano thinking: the task of deconstructing "ethics" and "politics" in order, paradoxically, to attend to the most radical ethical and political consequences of Derrida's writing. In "Marrano Spirit? . . . and Hispanism, or Responsibility in *2666*," Gareth Williams challenges the (somewhat ironic) title of the two seminars from which these essays emerged ("The Marrano Spirit: Derrida and Hispanism"—the title of the symposium) by describing the task of deconstructing (in) Hispanism as something that does not take place outside hegemonic disciplinary boundaries, but rather occupies a fold within: a withdrawal-without-exteriority. He then undertakes a close reading of "The Part about Archimboldi," the final section of Roberto Bolaño's *2666*, arguing that the character Reiter, a Nazi soldier-turned-writer, withdraws "majoritarian markers of historical imperial domination," entering a space that is neither properly ethical nor properly unethical. Williams names this withdrawal *becoming-marrano*, a concept that "applies as much to the nonmarrano as it does to the marrano, since the marrano enigma is not an identity but a refracting practice, a way of acting and surviving in the face of tyranny in such a way that murder and innocence are incommensurably conjoined as the most intimate wound of nonbelonging." Alberto Moreiras, in a similar vein, pursues the question of the "nonethical" together with the "infrapolitical" in his essay "Infrapolitical Derrida: The Ontic Determination of Politics beyond Empiricism." Revisiting the ethical philosophy of Emmanuel Levinas through Derrida's essay "Violence and Metaphysics," Moreiras identifies a strain of Derridean thought that subverts the logic of heliopolitics, or a politics of light, that stands at the center of Derrida's critique of Levinas's treatment of the Platonic sun. Such a shadow politics, marrano politics, or infrapolitics (in Moreiras's terminology) "would be the region of theoretical practice that solicits the constitutive opacity of the ethicopolitical relation—hence admits, for every practical decision, of no preceding political or ethical light to mark the path." In the volume's final essay, "Deconstruction and Its Precursors: Levinas and Borges after Derrida," Erin Graff Zivin considers two possible "precursors" of deconstruction, from two quite different traditions: Emmanuel Levinas and Jorge Luis Borges. The essay begins by evaluating the concept of the illegible demand (for reading) in the thought of Levinas and Derrida, suggesting that the most significant consequences of Levinas's writings can begin to be traced only "after" Derrida. Graff Zivin then argues, through a reading of Borges's "Kafka and His Precursors," that if literary and philosophical precursors can be determined retroactively and anachronistically (Borges "after" Derrida), intempestive reading—reading after whatever is untimely in the work before it—might serve as the condition of possibility for indisciplinary, marrano thinking.

NOTES

1. Recent publications on haunting and spectrality in Spanish and Latin American studies include works by María del Pilar Blanco and Patricia Keller, as well as a recent collection edited by Amanda L. Petersen and Alberto Ribas-Casasayas.

2. Marrano, converso, and crypto-Jewish history, including extensive debates over the nature of marrano faith and practice, have been amply treated by Miriam Bodian, David Graizbord, Jonathan I. Israel, Yosef Kaplan, Benzion Netanyahu, Anita Novinsky, Josê António Saraiva, Jonathan Schorsch, Nathan Wachtel, Yirmayahu Yovel, and Yosef Yerushalmi. In addition, Ronnie Perelis has studied marrano spiritual autobiography, focusing on narrative constructions of marrano subjectivity.

3. The conference paper "Marrano Universalism: Benjamin, Derrida, and Buck-Morss on the Condition of Universal Exile," which describes in summary form the argument developed in Agata Bielik-Robson's *Jewish Cryptotheologies*, appears on the blog *TelosSCOPE*.

4. Ricardo Forster elegantly describes the failure or fault line of the modern subject as marrano in nature: "La falla marrana atraviesa al sujeto moderno, lo ilumina con una nueva luz allí donde la luminosidad dominante parecía haber decretado definitivamente lo que quedaba de este lado del sentido y aquello otro que debía permanecer para siempre en las sombras de lo insustancial [The marrano fault line pierces the modern subject, illuminating it with a new light in the very place where the dominant luminosity appears to have decreed definitively what lay on this side of meaning and that which should forever remain in the shadows of the insubstantial]" (Forster, "La aventura marrana," 163).

5. Anne Norton draws attention to the marrano's "solitary interiority" as that which draws Derrida to this compelling figure: "Derrida has seen himself, as others have seen him, in the figure of the Marrano, one of the pretended converts hidden in the open after the *Reconquista*. The route his family travelled, from Spain to North Africa, was the route of many Marranos. So too was the route Derrida took later, form North Africa to Europe. Yet it is not the route travelled, nor the experience of exile, but the experience of a solitary interiority that marks the Marrano. The Marrano shelters a secret within, a secret that is at once the danger of death and the promise of salvation" (Norton, "Called to Bear Witness," 95).

6. For more on the link between marranismo and the concept of "Inquisitional logic," see my *Figurative Inquisitions* and "Beyond Inquisitional Logic."

7. See Ferrero Carracedo and de Peretti, de Peretti and Rocha, Richard, and Zerán.

8. "Deconstruction . . . has been practiced in Latin American Studies only on the rarest of occasions" (Levinson, *Ends of Literature*, 190).

WORKS CITED

Bielik-Robson, Agata. *Jewish Cryptotheologies of Late Modernity: Philosophical Marranos*. New York: Routledge, 2014.

———— "Marrano Universalism: Benjamin, Derrida, and Buck-Morss on the Condition of Universal Exile" *TelosSCOPE*. June 18, 2015. http://www.telospress.com/marrano-universalism-benjamin-derrida-and-buckmorss-on-the-condition-of-universal-exile/.

Blanco, María del Pilar. *Ghost-Watching American Modernity: Haunting, Landscape, and the Hemispheric Imagination*. New York: Fordham University Press, 2012.

Bodian, Miriam. *Dying in the Law of Moses: Crypto-Jewish Martyrdom in the Iberian World*. Bloomington: Indiana University Press, 2007.

Derrida, Jacques. *Aporias*. 1992. Translated by Thomas Dutoit. Stanford: Stanford University Press, 1993.

———. *Archive Fever.* 1995. Translated by Eric Prenowitz. Chicago: University of Chicago Press, 1996.

———. *Circumfession.* 1991. Translated by Geoffrey Bennington. In *Jacques Derrida,* by Geoffrey Bennington and Jacques Derrida. Chicago: University of Chicago Press, 1993.

———. "History of the Lie: Prolegomena." 1993. In *Without Alibi,* edited and translated by Peggy Kamuf, 28–70. Stanford: Stanford University Press, 2002.

———. "Passions: 'An Oblique Offering.'" Translated by David Wood. In *On the Name,* edited by Thomas Detoit, translated by David Wood, John P. Leavey Jr., and Ian McLeod, 3–31. Stanford: Stanford University Press, 1995.

———. *Specters of Marx: The State of Debt, the Work of Mourning, and the New International.* Translated by Peggy Kamuf. New York: Routledge, 1994.

———. "Typewriter Ribbon: Limited Ink (2)." In *Without Alibi,* edited and translated by Peggy Kamuf, 71–160. Stanford: Stanford University Press, 2002.

de Peretti, Cristina, and Delmiro Rocha. "Las *Spanish-speaking Connections* de Derrida." Rio de Janeiro: *Alea* 17 (2015): 78–91.

Fathy, Safaa, dir. *D'ailleurs, Derrida.* First Run / Icarus Films, 1999.

Ferrero Carracedo, Luis, and Cristina de Peretti. "La Recepción en España del pensamiento de Jacques Derrida." Madrid: *Revista de Filosofía* 6 (1983): 148–60.

Forster, Ricardo. "La aventura marrana en la constitución del sujeto moderno: Claves para comprender la entrada del judaísmo en la época de la secularización." In *Mesianismo, nihilismo y redención: De Abraham a Spinoza, de Marx a Benjamin,* edited by Ricardo Forster and Diego Tatián, 143–203. Buenos Aires: Altamira, 2005.

Graff Zivin, Erin. "Aporias of Marranismo: Sabina Berman's *En el nombre de Dios* and Jom Tob Azulay's *O Judeu.*" *CR: The New Centennial Review* 12, no. 3 (2012): 187–216.

———. "Beyond Inquisitional Logic, or Toward an An-archaeological Latin Americanism." *CR: The New Centennial Review* 14, no. 1 (2014): 195–211.

———. *Figurative Inquisitions: Conversion, Torture, and Truth in the Luso-Hispanic Atlantic.* Evanston, Ill.: Northwestern University Press, 2014.

———. "Marrano Secrets, or, Misunderstanding Literature." *CR: The New Centennial Review* 14, no. 3 (2014): 75–91.

Graizbord, David. *Souls in Dispute: Converso Identities in Iberia and the Jewish Diaspora, 1580–1700.* Philadelphia: University of Pennsylvania Press, 2004.

Hammerschlag, Sarah. "Poetics of the Broken Tablet." In *The Trace of God: Derrida and Religion*, edited by Edward Baring and Peter E. Gordon, 59–71. New York: Fordham University Press, 2014.

Israel, Jonathan I. *Diasporas within a Diaspora: Jews, Crypto-Jews and the World Maritime Empires (1540–1740)*. Leiden: Brill, 2002.

Kaplan, Yosef. *Jews and Conversos: Studies in Society and the Inquisition.* Jerusalem: Hebrew University Magnes Press, 1985.

Keller, Patricia. *Ghostly Landscapes: Film, Photography, and the Aesthetics of Haunting in Contemporary Spanish Culture.* Toronto: University of Toronto Press, 2016.

Kleinberg, Ethan. "Not Yet Marrano: Levinas, Derrida, and the Ontology of Being Jewish." In *The Trace of God: Derrida and Religion*, edited by Edward Baring and Peter E. Gordon, 39–58. New York: Fordham University Press, 2014.

Levinson, Brett. *The Ends of Literature: The Latin American "Boom" in the Neoliberal Marketplace.* Stanford: Stanford University Press, 2002.

Netanyahu, Benzion. *The Marranos of Spain from the Late 14th to the Early 16th Century.* New York: American Academy for Jewish Research, 1966.

Norton, Anne. "Called to Bear Witness: Derrida, Muslims, and Islam." In *The Trace of God: Derrida and Religion*, edited by Edward Baring and Peter E. Gordon, 88–109. New York: Fordham University Press, 2014.

Novinsky, Anita. *Cristãos Novos na Bahia*. São Paulo, Brazil: Universidade de São Paulo & Editora Perspectiva, 1970.

Perelis, Ronnie. "Blood and Spirit: Paternity, Fraternity and Religious Self-fashioning in Luis de Carvajal's Spiritual Autobiography." *Estudios Interdisciplinarios de América Latina y el Caribe* 23, no. 1 (2012): 77–98.

———. *Narratives from the Sephardic Atlantic: Blood and Faith.* Bloomington: Indiana University Press, 2016.

Ribas-Casasayas, Alberto, and Amanda L. Petersen. *Ghostly Hauntings in Contemporary Transhispanic Narratives.* Lanham, MD: Rowman and Littlefield; Lewisburg, Pa.: Bucknell University Press, 2015.

Richard, Nelly, et al. "Debate con Jacques Derrida: Los fantasmas de Marx." *Revista de Crítica Cultural* 12 (1996).

Saraiva, António José. *The Marrano Factory: The Portuguese Inquisition and Its New Christians, 1536–1765.* Translated by H. P. Salomon and I. S. D. Sassoon. Leiden: Brill, 2001.

Schorsch, Jonathan. *Swimming the Christian Atlantic: Judeoconversos, Afroiberians and Amerindians in the Seventeenth Century.* Leiden: Brill, 2009.

Villacañas, José Luis. "Spinoza: Democracia y subjetividad marrana." *Política Común: A Journal of Thought* 1 (2011): 55–86.

Wachtel, Nathan. 2001. *The Faith of Remembrance: Marrano Labyrinths*. Translated by Nikki Halpern. Philadelphia: University of Pennsylvania Press, 2013.

Yerushalmi, Yosef. *From Spanish Court to Italian Ghetto: Isaac Cardoso: A Study in Seventeenth-Century Marranism and Jewish Apologetics*. St. Louis, Mo.: Washington University Press, 1971.

Yovel, Yirmiyahu. *The Other Within: The Marranos: Split Identity and Emerging Modernity*. Princeton: Princeton University Press, 2009.

Zerán, Faride. "Derrida y el tiempo de la confusión." In *Desacatos al desencanto: Ideas para cambiar de milenio*, 147–60. Santiago, Chile: LOM Ediciones, 1997.

PART I

Marrano Indisciplinarity

CHAPTER I

Cervantes on "Derrida": Hispanism in the Open

Jacques Lezra

What I said made no law, but was rather a promise to bite my tongue
whenever I slandered. Things now, however, aren't as rigorous,
nor are matters held to the same literal sense, as of old. Today you
make a law, and tomorrow you break it, and perhaps it's best so.
One promises just now to reject one's vices, and falls straightaway
into other, greater ones. It's one thing to praise the scourge [*la
disciplina*] and quite another to lash oneself with it: sooner said than
done. Let the devil bite himself, for I don't want to bite myself.

—MIGUEL DE CERVANTES, "EL COLOQUIO DE LOS PERROS,"
in *Novelas Ejemplares*

I would not want to let myself be imprisoned in a culture of
the secret, which however I do rather like, as I like that figure
of the Marrano, which keeps popping up in all my texts.

—JACQUES DERRIDA, *Paper Machine*

Let's play a dangerous game.[1] Let's imagine a primal scene for Hispanism.
The game is dangerous because it tends to be played in order to grant the
origin a determinative quality, as if to say that *there*, at the scene where this
event occurred, are set the rules according to which we, our discipline, will
develop, the rules according to which we will see our origin, or judge them
to be the true origins of our discursive practices. But it is not self-evident
what makes a scene "primal" or originary—in fact, we enter a circle immediately, since the designation of a mythological scene as primary with
respect to a discipline or a discursive or institutional practice is largely an
effect of the discipline, or at any rate it is the sort of speech-act understand-
able to that discipline, articulated in its lexicon, judged to be true or false
in accord with the protocols that this discipline has set in place: It is only
on the condition that there is such a thing as Hispanism, for instance, that
we can point to its founding moment and say, with assurance, yes, that
is indeed primary, that scene captures a moment of origination; we can
trace the primary features of Hispanism to this moment. What it is that

is primary about a primal scene is always secondary to the discipline that takes account of it. At the same time, who or what it is that determines which scene is originary or primal is not self-evident. The game of imagining primal disciplinary scenes tends to be played so as to grant primacy with respect to the primal scene to its designator, to the person or institution who, being the product of the disciplinary conventions, nevertheless seizes them to arrogate to himself a sovereign position with respect to the field in which he or she is embedded. Who or what determines is perhaps given in the scene, or perhaps not, but in either case it's a gesture of force, an act of will, a sovereign decision, a coup de main, to assert that yes, here, this event is primal for us, for our discipline.[2]

An underground current of counterdisciplinarity or nondisciplinarity flows alongside and against this pervasive and recognizable account of the relation between discipline or frame, and epistemological object. This underground current, always also flowing across and roiling the narcissistic formal circuit in which the disciplinary object, subject, and protocol are formed, has had different names when it's had names—deconstruction is one of them; so is philology, in the specific sense that Nietzsche gave the word (which is also, mutatis mutandis, the sense it has recently for Werner Hamacher).[3] The term that some of us have been using in our scholarship and the term that draws us together here, the term "marrano," should be understood not just as a figure for a counteridentity or for a register or mode of thought that contests an established metaphysical, onto-theological tradition but also in a restricted sense as a logical operator that serves to bring *play*, that is, unfoundedness, the substitutability of contents, terms, and elements, in brief, *transvaluation*, paradoxically to the center of disciplinary structure.[4] ("Paradoxical" because, in principle, a "center" cannot be exchanged or substituted for any other element or position of a field or discipline, any more than a "primary scene" can be, in the fields of our recollections and our fantasies: That's their secret.) This volume is calling this counterdisciplinarity "the marrano specter."

Let's play the game. We're looking for an account that knots together the will, an epistemic-cultural field, the problem of positioning a spectator-critic with respect to that field, the matter of the standing and value of his or her discourse as it concerns that epistemic-cultural field, and a reflection on the obscurity and danger of origins. Here's the story that I find. A young boy of mysterious origins and background takes up with two passing students, serves them, befriends and studies with them, and becomes famous for his intelligence. He leaves the quiet of the university, travels, briefly pursues a career as a soldier, but finally returns to Salamanca after visiting Italy. He becomes there the object of affection for "una dama de todo rumbo y manejo," or, as Walter Kelly's 1846 translation puts it, "one of those ladies who belong to all the points of the compass; she was besides well furnished with devices of every colour," thus a spectacular and, we understand, loose-moraled woman.[5] This "dama" falls hard for our hero; she "made her desires clear to him"; and then, seeing that she cannot conquer his will, she seeks other means to ensnare him. So, "following the counsel of a morisca, she gave Tomás a philtre of the sort they call bewitched [*aconsejada de una morisca, en un membrillo toledano dio a Tomás unos destos que llaman hechizos*]." Tomás is, of course, Tomás Rodaja, the protagonist of Cervantes's *novela ejemplar* "El licenciado Vidriera." The result of this little scheme is not to alter his will and desires, but to drive him mad—"mad, with the strangest madness seen among madnesses till then [*loco de la más estraña locura que entre las locuras hasta entonces se había visto*]": He believes himself to be made of glass, and, newly named "el licenciado Vidriera" (a "vidriera" being a glass display case) he wanders the streets of Salamanca from encounter to encounter, answering questions with greater freedom and intelligence than when, a mere embodied human, "heavy and earthen [*pesado y terrestre*]" (277), he walked the town sane. Two years later Vidriera is cured, converted to sanity by "a friar of the Order of Saint Jerome, who had special skill and knowledge [*gracia y ciencia*] in making mute people understand and express themselves after a fashion [*en hacer que los mudos entendiesen y en cierta manera hablasen*]" (299). Discipline is restored; the expression of a pathology, truth-telling in the streets, now becomes private practice: "What you used to ask me in the city squares, ask me now in my house [*Lo que solíades preguntarme en las plazas preguntádmelo ahora en mi casa*]," the now sane, but distraught and hungry *licenciado* tells the crowds following him (299). For Rueda, as he is now called, finds himself much less successful as a sane and private scholar than as a notorious itinerant, public, mad wit. Starving, he leaves the court at last, and dies abroad, "famous, in death, for having been a wise and exceptionally brave soldier."[6]

Cervantes's mysterious story has plagued criticism and scholarship for years. How are we to understand it? Why can't we understand it? The *novela* asks its readers to imagine Vidriera as something like the embodiment of peripatetic truth, of the function of truth-telling wandering, like Diogenes with a lantern, in the open, casting an occasional light into the shadows of social obscurantism, ideology, and self-deception.[7] So he and his fate can pass, I think, for representatives of disciplinarity and disciplinarization: a wild will-to-truth, cast into the open, pathologized, free to wander and to comment and to produce, paratactically, punctual observations regarding the world's confusions; this wild will-to-truth is brought back, converted, to a productive sanity, brought in from the open to the halls of court or the ranks of the army, ideologized, consensualized, capitalized.[8]

Say, then, that we take Vidriera's story as a sort of allegory of disciplinarity: a myth, if you will. It may be—it seems not improbable—that contemporary academic disciplines have trouble, specific sorts of trouble, taking account of these constitutive, mythological scenes. Stay with our story, though. How does Hispanism's specific difficulty in accounting for the scene of its origination work? What might this specific difficulty tell us about this contemporary field?

Set aside the obvious problems that arise from the fact that Vidriera's conversion, or cure, results in his exile, in the loss, for himself and for his society, for the court and for the university, of the peripatetic and uncontrolled function of truth-telling. Cervantes's allegory allows us to approach what we call disciplinarity slightly differently than we are accustomed to, in the wake of the Enlightenment, when modern disciplinarity seems to take shape. The model of disciplinarity that the modern university tends to rely on, more or less without question, is an autopoetic one: Those objects of study and interpretation we can understand are the ones recognized by the disciplinary lexicon as objects; what counts as an act of understanding, or interpretation, or positioning, is reflexively given in that lexicon; our authority to make judgments regarding the objects before us derives from the discipline, which in turn generates both the objects and the positions from which they can be designated as such, evaluated, interpreted, positioned taxonomically. Whether this or that epistemological object a discipline takes into account squares with it or not, that it can be identified *as* an object of thought in and for the discipline confirms the epistemic comprehensiveness *of* the discipline, and the standing of its practitioners. At this level, any epistemological object tells, or bears stamped upon it in ghostly characters, the story of its becoming-an-object for a particular framework, world picture, or discipline. For these and in these—frameworks, worlds, disciplines—these epistemological objects are equivalent inasmuch as they can be substituted among themselves: They all share the quality of *being* such objects, and with reference to this quality they are interchangeable. Disciplines, in short and to flatten the argument to this point, are structures, and in particular they are what Derrida famously referred to, in his 1966 lecture "Structure, Sign, and Play in the Discourse of the Human Sciences," as structures whose play is limited (organized, balanced, oriented) by the operation of a center, in this case, the central role played by the correlation between the objects of the discipline and the value- and meaning-producing mechanisms of the discipline. This central correlation is sovereign with respect to the discipline that it commands: It lies, Derrida says about "centered" structures in general, "paradoxically, *within* the structure and *outside* of it."[9] This correlation opens the "play" of the structure and also closes it; it is the point at which "the substitution of contents, elements, terms, is no longer possible . . . [it] is *forbidden* . . . [it] has always remained *interdicted*" (279).

In a restricted sense, the difficulties any discipline encounters in understanding, or placing, or valuing certain texts, objects, or ideas or identities flow from the ways in which these resist becoming allegories of the discipline's reflexive value-form. (If we accept the description I give above, then we may say that the story of the epistemological object's becoming-an-object for a particular framework, world picture, or discipline turns out to be incoherent, or at least in part unreadable, for these frameworks, etc.) The study and uses of Derrida's work, for instance, to the extent that such study and uses have acquired a systematic, institutional, or disciplinary character over the past half-century, is one such structure. (Systematic, institutional, disciplinary: conferences, biographies, films, the publication and translation of his seminars, a small library of works devoted to Derrida's work, protocols for its study, lexicons, conventional and disciplining accounts of his concepts, and so on. The fashioning of "Derrida" from the rough stuff to which Jacques Derrida signed his name.) It is highly consequential that the content about which this Derridological discipline turns resolutely seeks to show the metaphysical presuppositions *of* structured disciplines: Something like what Derrida calls an "autoimmune" process lodges at the heart of the structured, disciplinary encounter with Derrida's work. Say we looked synoptically at the corpus, as Derrida so often does himself (in gestures we could then call simultaneously autodisciplinary and estranging, and ignoring for now the body of work's immunological resistance to such structuring, synoptic, and resolutely metaphysical gestures). We'd be after a central term providing "a fundamental ground . . . that very thing [*cela même*] within a structure, which governs the structure, while escaping structurality." Or rather, we would be casting a synoptic eye over "Derrida" with the hope of producing or unveiling "a series of substitutions of center for center" forming the corpus, giving his work the shape, heft, dignity, and sovereign coherence of an epistemological object thinkable "as a linked chain of determinations of the center. Successively, and in a regulated fashion," in "Derrida"'s corpus as such "the center receives different forms or names." Think of the declensions of "center," from its treatment here, in "Structure, Sign, and Play" in 1966: supplement, *pharmakon*, *tympan*, woman, spirit, trace, writing, *différance*, autoimmunity, translation, marranismo. What the academy calls "Derrida" "is the history of these metaphors and metonymies."

Hispanism is another such "centered" structure, of course—more obviously a "discipline" than the study of "Derrida"'s work, but similarly machinic in its autopoetics, that is, in producing epistemological objects, legitimation processes, value-systems, and identities. The differences are obvious, but nevertheless I've rather tendentiously brought these two disciplines into contact just now by adding marranismo to the "linked chain" of metonyms or metaphors that give shape to "Derrida" today. My claim is stronger still, and perhaps more perverse. What makes the "center" (and its metonyms, including marranismo) different from every other epistemological object in the disciplinary field is its peculiar topology and its peculiar temporality, its play: inside and out; arche as well as telos; identifiable and not; valuable and not; exposed as well as secret; thus self-identical, and not. Thus it is not the "center" that stands as the literal term from which fly and flow the armies of metaphors and metonyms that shape and unshape the metaphysics of structure for Derrida and in "Derrida," but rather the term that names the secret and defective center *of* Hispanism: *marrano*, the last term in Derrida's list, the term that returns for him, to him, as a sort of "obsession" (that is Derrida's word, in the film *D'ailleurs, Derrida*; here is a question the film's director, Safaa Fathy, asks, regarding the scenes shot in Toledo, in Spain: "Why do we find the figure of the marrano in this inner courtyard of the ancient Jewish quarter of Toledo, the place of an origin and of its exile?")[10]

To show you what I mean, let me return to Cervantes's *novela*—which I take to stand at, and as, the tactile, untouchable center of Hispanism.

Let's observe from the start that the difficulties Hispanism has had in reading Cervantes's *novela* are symptoms of the difficulties it has had more broadly in understanding itself as a structure. These difficulties might then be said to flow, in the restricted case of "El licenciado Vidriera," from that work's unwillingness (it may seem sloppy to speak of a *novela*'s "will"—in this case, it turns out, the phrasing is precise) to become a proper epistemic object, neither conforming to the protocols the discipline establishes for valuing and interpreting works, nor shedding a reflexive value and coherence on those protocols, on that discipline, and on its subjects and practitioners. Vidriera's condition—"maddened with the strangest madness ever till then remarked among all sorts of madness [*loco de la más estraña locura que entre las locuras hasta entonces se había visto*]"—is strange almost to the point of singularity, the strangest of the strange and estranging forms of madness. And like Bartleby's, another singular character, his condition is strangest inasmuch as he *both* lies, or wanders, outside and inside every frame at our disposal and at the story's disposal for thinking and placing him, *and also* does not assume a sovereign position with regard to such frames or disciplines. We're operating on the level of a strong analogy: just as the central character's madness pulls him out from the cover of university, court, law chamber, army, and even the dress and custom of other humans, and out into "las plazas," into the open, where he bitingly exposes the truth of his society's compromises, clichés, hypocrisies, and so on—so too the *novela* that bears his name wanders away from the discipline to which it appears as an object for understanding or evaluation, into the open.

But this is still too abstract, with respect both to our story and to the story of Hispanism. We could be talking about "Bartleby" as much as we could be about "Vidriera."

Vidriera's strangeness, his in-discipline, is tied, pathologically, to the cultural register from which it springs. His own origin may be mysterious, but the origin of his madness and its somatic consequences, its symptomatology and slow presentation over months of illness, are explicit, laid out narratively with juridical and medical precision. The poison that the morisca provides the "loose and wayward damsel [*dama de todo rumbo y manejo*]" or, as we have seen, "one of those ladies who belong to all the points of the compass; she was besides well furnished with devices of every colour," passes into Tomás Rodaja's body in a "membrillo toledano," a quince compote. This culturally overdetermined object replaces, but also serves to capture or convert, Rodaja's genealogical origins. *Membrillo* has become since Cervantes's time an eponym for any sort of sticky compote and not just one made from quince, so that we can speak of *membrillo de manzana*, or *de guayaba*, and so on. We'll see, at the close, just what else *this membrillo* can come to suggest as well. Our little epistemic object, our *membrillo toledano* provides both the benefit of lucidity and the poison of madness and social death—hence the double sense of the word used to describe those who provide such poisons and the effect of the poisons themselves: "veneficio," which echoes both the Latin *bene-ficium*, a pharmaceutical that does good, and *veneno*, poison. The analogy expands here, like poison flowing across membranes: The analogy works now between the *membrillo* and the *licenciado*, between objects within the story and the characters that these objects then convert into strange, dried objects wandering through the story's streets; this in turn becomes like the effect the story may claim to have on its early modern readership; and this effect in turn resembles, at a different level entirely, the way the story acts on and for Hispanism, where it serves as an epistemic object constitutive of the disciplinary structure itself. At the center of the *novela's* plot, this beneficent-maleficent object, the *membrillo*, serves the purpose that Vidriera himself serves with respect to the society represented in "El licenciado Vidriera"—the purpose of driving it mad, of showing it singularities it cannot countenance, of making manifest the conditions on which the truth can come into the open, and not wander "in the shadows, sneaking under cover of rooftops, chased and mistreated [*a sombra de tejados, corrida y maltratada*]." This too—the formal analogy continues—is the purpose served by a work like "El licenciado Vidriera" for Cervantes's readership: it is a *novela ejemplar* whose example is both beneficent and malevolent.[11] If literary culture had followed its example, if it had remained in the open of the poison the story offers, if it had followed the example set by Vidriera rather than the beneficent example offered by the cured Rueda or the naïve Rodaja, Spain would have been a more convivial home to one highly heterodox group of Cervantes's readers—to Sterne, to Diderot, to Marx, to Freud. Finally, the *novela* unhinges the discipline that seeks to take it as a proper epistemic object: It is a sort of *membrillo toledano* with respect to the study of culture, of the culture from which Spain develops, and the intellectual culture from which Hispanism develops. Cervantes's *novela* maddens the critic; it drives him or her into the open; it exposes the critic. The story sets modern thought wandering, unhoused, on errands of accidental truth-telling, through established and institutionalized landscapes, a danger to all and to itself.

Let me remind you of the game we are playing. I offered "El licenciado Vidriera" as an exemplary allegory for disciplinarity and, in its stubborn resistance to becoming an epistemic object for disciplining, as an allegory of the underground current of counterdisciplinarity we are calling marranismo or "the marrano specter." The story works well to this double end because it knits together the will, *la voluntad*; an epistemic-cultural field; the problem of positioning a spectator-critic with respect to that field; the matter of the standing and value of his or her discourse as it concerns that epistemic-cultural field; and a reflection on the obscurity and danger of origins. I offered "El licenciado Vidriera," then, as an object for thinking about disciplinarity and about the underground current of counterdisciplinarity we might be calling "the marrano specter." But the matter is more specific: It is *Hispanism* that turns about the strange, autoimmune process set in play by our story's *membrillo toledano*. What, then, is "Hispanic," if anything, about "El licenciado Vidriera"? What about it is marrano or "Derridean"?

The three ways that twentieth-century philosophical and historical culture provides for identifying what is characteristically Hispanic about *Homo hispanus*—positions with three names attached to them, José Ortega y Gasset, Claudio Sánchez Albornoz, and Américo Castro—are braided together about the set of problems that Cervantes's story places on display. The notional encounter between the three extends over the period from the publication of Ortega's *España invertebrada* in 1921, through the appearance of Castro's *España en su historia* in 1948 and *La realidad histórica de España* a decade later, and ends perhaps with the publication of Sánchez Albornoz's *España, un enigma histórico*, in 1957. Evidently, this encounter has fuzzy chronological borders, stretching back to earlier reflections on the Spanish character, and lasting to our day, when the debate regarding the specific quality of Hispanic identity in Spain and elsewhere is the province of extreme nationalists like Pío Moa, or administrators and demographers intent on charting the rise of Hispanism in the Anglophone world. *Homo hispanus*, for Ortega, is an ancient creature, who exercises will, yes, but without a proper external object on which to exercise it, just the shadowy awareness of possessing a unified character yet to be defined. This shadowy want-of-object becomes the desire for empire; it is the common lack-of-object that constitutes the commonality of the Spanish people and drives their expansive will. The expansion of Spain into America and the practices of Christianization and conversion that attend this expansion and support it are the effect of the lack of object; the empire is the compensatory device for a will, a national and an individual character, deprived of an adequate object. For Castro, the Spanish character takes shape in the fraught mix and dangerous dance among the three cultures of the Book, whose long tense cohabitation over eight centuries produces the modern Spanish character, whatever it may be. And for Sánchez Albornoz, *Homo hispanus* precedes the Arabo-Muslim invasion of Spain; subsists in a medieval, Christian Visigothic quiet; persists in the hills of Asturias; reconquers, expels, and in doing so maintains a character set before Judaism and Islam entered the Peninsula.

The specifics of this debate over *el Ser de España* are well enough known. The strange, compelling, nationalist, Castilianist bases it sits on seem to us archaic today, dangerous, so out of step with the modern day-to-day life of Spain and Latin America as to be barely worth recalling, even as a moment in the cultural history of the twentieth century. And so it would be, perhaps, if it weren't that Hispanism and Latin Americanism still bear the ghostly marks of the debate. They inherit its identitarian grammar and take their compensatory shape from it. Everything, we might say, about the two disciplines flows from the encounter with this *membrillo toledano*, or from the effort *not* to encounter the strange, poisoned fruit that plays at governing at the center of the story, and at the secret center of Spanish modernity. Compensatory: yes, *Homo hispanus* stands paternally behind today's Hispanism and today's Latin Americanism—but he stands on ground, in the street, in the place of another center, substituting for it, erecting himself in the sovereign and secret spot from which he has sought to drive Cervantes's undisciplined madman. The secret of the secret, the secret "object" for which *Homo hispanus* can never quite substitute? This little member that the Judeo-Christian-Islamic *veneficio* provides; the strange charm intended to bend the young man's will: not a substance, not a body, but a wandering relation among identities (the Abrahamic identities, let's say), a wandering, like the truth in Cervantes's story, unhoused, harried, mistreated. *Homo hispanus* either refuses the poison and the benefits that this *membrillo toledano* offers and affirms his identity in this refusal, or willfully absorbs it and places it at the center of his identity. In either case, *Homo hispanus* acts to structure *Hispania*, and Hispanism, about a central, sovereign identity which, inasmuch as it is not an identity but a wandering and contingent relation, is itself excluded from substitution, from play, from transvaluation.

And what, finally, is this strange object-that-is-not-an-object, this object-as-relation, the center of a story that itself becomes the center of an allegory about the relation between the will, knowledge, national identity, and disciplinarity, a story that lies behind the story of contemporary Hispanism? Where does the *membrillo toledano* come from? As to the last question, we know, from other moments in Cervantes's work (from other sources as well, of course)—including the famous prologue to the second part of *Don Quixote*—that the city of Toledo is indeed in early Hispanic modernity the mythographic point of contact between the three cultures of the Book. (We know also, from Safaa Fathy and Jacques Derrida's essay and film *D'ailleurs, Derrida*, that for Derrida

> Toledo especially guarded and kept a memory, to all appearances orphaned and unattached, which let itself be appropriated and which Derrida had already made his own: the memory of the Spanish *marrano* of the 14th and 15th centuries. The Jew who, converting to Catholicism, nevertheless keeps his faith secretly. . . . Phantom memory of the revenant, dramatic and novelesque, which Spain has given us [*dont l'Espagne nous a fait don*], flowing from these abandoned, even defunct, places, and from these ruins, in recollection of a lost origin.[12]

The broken edges of our discipline: What we *know* about the *membrillo*'s sources comes to us from Cervantes's time and before—philology establishes, names a given corpus—but also from its future, from its outcome, for instance in Derrida's encounter with Toledo.) Everything about contemporary Hispanism flows from the rejection of Toledo, from refusing Toledo's gift to Spain and Spain's gift, its *don*, to "us," the poison that this *membrillo toledano* offers to the will of an organized, membered, structure, of a society, a discipline, a collection of objects and identities structured about a central member.

What, again, is this strange object, the center of a story that becomes the center of an allegory about the relation between the will, knowledge, touch, and disciplinarity? It turns out that the beneficent-maleficent little object is not a single object at all, and for that reason may not have an identity at all, in a classic sense. I've been describing it as a wandering relation, but perhaps not with sufficient stress on the paradox this entails: Relation prior to the settled disciplinary objects or identities related. The consequences of this rather scholastic-sounding paradox are grave. I have been delighting you with the relation between a society composed of members, an organic society arising on the shoulders of *Homo hispanus*, as his fantasy, as the product of his sword and his gesture. It is a fantasy imagined in political-philosophical treatises from Aristotle through Hobbes and on to Spanish National Catholicism. This is what Sebastián de Covarrubias, the great early modern lexicographer, says about the object at the center of the structure, and of the discipline that I have been imagining for us. "Membrillo," writes Covarrubias, "Quince: a common fruit. In Latin it is known as *malum Cydonium*, from a Cretan village called Cidon. . . . The etymology of *membrillo* is understood by some to derive from the diminutive of the word *membrum*, for the likeness most of the fruits have with the female genital organs [*fruta conocida, de Latín se llama malum Cydonium, de vna villa de Creta llamada Cidon . . . La etimología de membrillo traen algunos del diminutiuo de la palabra membrum, por cierta semejança, que tienen los mas dellos con el miembro genital y femineo*]." This "likeness," *cierta semejança, que tienen los mas dellos,* is symptomatically unstable. "*Membrum,*" Covarrubias writes, "*vulgo significat virilia, seu pudenda.*"[13] *Virilia* as well as "miembro genital y femineo." We now have a fuller sense of the transvaluation of the object, its reconstruction as a relational, autoimmune process prior to any object positioned in a disciplinary field, that can be effected by the marrano specter, by and in this counterdisciplinarity that runs like poison inside and next to the beneficent and exemplary objects from which cultures derive their value, their histories, and their self-understanding. The task that Cervantes's character sets on display for us, which Covarrubias's marvelously divided definitions exemplify, and which Derrida carries on in philosophy many years later, is not to substitute a diminutive little member in place of a greater one, not to find or cook up a *membrillo* to take the place of the organic *membrum* that broods at and as the center, rising in phallic sovereignty over the field of epistemological objects whose play it regulates. "El licenciado Vidriera" does not invite us to choose another form of disciplinary interpretation over an autopoetic Hispanism, Latin Americanism, or over the disciplinary study of "Derrida." Rather, Cervantes's story and the deconstructions it makes possible allow the wandering, relational play of undecidability to poison the identity of the object. Their strange, exacting discipline—which we cannot choose to ignore, any more than Cervantes's Berganza can choose not to let his tongue wander from story to slander: not by abjectly praising the scourge, *la disciplina*, and not by disciplining ourselves with it—requires that we transvalue epistemological objects and their subjects and thus raise, as the "proper" shape of disciplinary knowledge and of the sovereignties formed by and in disciplines, what Derrida calls "the species of non-species, under the unformed form, mute, infantile and terrifying, of monstrosity." Or, we can now say, of the marrano.

NOTES

1. My epigraphs are from Miguel de Cervantes, "El Coloquio de los perros," in *Novelas Ejemplares*, 570, and Jacques Derrida, *Paper Machine*, 162. Except where noted all translations are my own.

2. My arguments regarding the discipline of Cervantic studies, in Jacques Lezra, "The Disciplining of don Quijote and the Discipline of Literary Studies."

3. I am thinking of the two "verbal gestures" that (for Hamacher) philology follows and permits—a disciplining and disciplinary gesture "defining a textual corpus according to its boundaries"; and a second gesture that "generates border conflicts in microscopic and macroscopic regions . . . colliding." Werner Hamacher, *Minima Philologica*, 129.

4. In the wake of Derrida's manifold uses of the term, the bibliography on appropriations of *marrano* is burgeoning. Some of the contributors to this volume, Erin Graff Zivin and Alberto Moreiras in particular, take up the term in a frame offered by Ricardo Forster. See Ricardo Foster, "La ficción marrana: Claves para una historia a contrapelo de la subjetividad moderna." I am thinking of Erin Graff Zivin, "Politics against Ethics" and "Aporias of Marranismo: Sabina Berman's *En el nombre de Dios* and Jom Tob Azulay's *O*

Judeu." See her *Figurative Inquisitions: Conversion, Torture, and Truth in the Luso-Hispanic Atlantic*: "The marrano subject matters to us—here, now—because it signals, from the beginning, the *other side* of reunification, nationalism, and colonialism, as well as the necessary failure of these political, religious, and identitary projects. Marranismo works on a number of levels, within distinct spheres (the cultural, the socioeconomic, the religious, the metaphysical, the political, the symbolic), and its effect can be felt across the Atlantic: not only because of the marrano participation in early voyages of conquest in the Americas, but also in light of the conversion and subjugation of indigenous communities in the colonies" (23). See Alberto Moreiras, "Common Political Democracy: The Marrano Register," and the related concept of "infrapolitics" that Moreiras begins to develop in *Línea de sombra: El no sujeto de lo político*. As concerns Derrida's use of the term in particular, see Peggy Kamuf, *To Follow: The Wake of Jacques Derrida*, especially chapter 10, "Stunned." An effort to understand marranismo as a characteristic specifically of Jewish philosophy, including Derrida's work, in Agata Bielik-Robson, *Jewish Cryptotheologies of Late Modernity: Philosophical Marranos*. For a complementary position, see Ethan Kleinberg's "Not Yet Marrano: Levinas, Derrida, and the Ontology of Being Jewish," in *The Trace of God: Derrida and Religion*. An approach more consonant with Moreiras's, in Marc Goldschmit, *L'hypothèse du Marrane: Le théâtre judéo-chrétien de la pensée politique*: "The *marrano* hypothesis announces itself as the being, the unconscious, and the deconstruction of present democracy—and its future, and its specter beyond its being" (11). For my own preliminary thoughts on the marrano matter, see Jacques Lezra, "Marranes que nous sommes?"

5. I cite in Spanish from Miguel de Cervantes, "El licenciado Vidriera," in García López, ed., *Novelas ejemplares*; henceforth, page numbers in my text refer to this edition. Here, from page 275. Kelly's English for "de todo rumbo y manejo" is from *The Exemplary Novels of Miguel de Cervantes Saavedra*, 94. Harriet de Onís is more circumspect. Her translation of "Master Glass" refers to "a woman versed in wiles and intrigue." In *Six Exemplary Novels*, Miguel de Cervantes, 70. On Cervantes's phrase "de todo rumbo y manejo," I find illuminating Mauricio Molho and Felipe Ruan's observations. Ruan writes that the phrase "de todo rumbo y manejo," in Kelly's translation "one of those ladies who belong to all the points of the compass... well furnished with devices of every colour," "provokes the most intense crisis of the story. . . . We find ourselves facing a force of great mobility ('de todo manejo,' capable of moving around or being guided anywhere), which makes us consider the possibility that in the phrase 'de todo rumbo y manejo' we may find the operating principle of Cervantes's discourse in this story." Felipe Ruan, "Carta de guía, carto-grafía: Fallas y fisuras en 'El licenciado

Vidriera.'" See also Mauricio Molho, "Una dama de todo rumbo y manejo:
Para una lectura de 'El licenciado Vidriera.'"

6. Vicente Pérez de Leon, *Cervantes y el Cuarto misterio*, cleverly describes the *novela* as a "walking narrative artifice, an interactive book of
aphorisms," 542. See also his conclusion: "Tomás's end manages to bolster
the exemplary frame that the story had preserved through his life, in a linear
fashion, until his madness. The circular structure closes when the initial
prophetic ending fulfills itself with the protagonist's death in Flanders" (549).
More than "bolster" the exemplary framework, though, Tomás's disastrous
end would seem to undermine it.

7. Thus Juan Pablo Gil-Osle, *Amistades imperfectas: del humanismo a la
ilustración con Cervantes*: "In 'El licenciado Vidriera' we don't find merely an
open, disclosed, sincere man, but something much greater: a glassy totality,
a glassed man. . . . The transparent breast, open to view, expands to become
the total transparency of a hypothetical glass man. This metonymy inscribes
a reference to the language of *amicitia* (*qua* part) and to licentiate Rueda's
illness (*qua* whole). This is the disenchanted mention of *amicitia* inscribed
in the metaphor of transparency, proper to a society of baroque obfusca-
tions" (123).

8. For an interpretation of the *novela* as social critique, see William H.
Clamurro, "Hacia una lectura ideológica de las *Novelas ejemplares*: El caso de
'El licenciado Vidriera.'" Clamurro understands the *novela* to be a "concrete
demonstration, direct as well as indirect, of the decadence and failures of
a social world, a culture, and individual human imagination, in which the
contradictions and *aporias* of political ideology and social beliefs (and, in
particular, the matter of personal identity *as* a member of, or as someone
excluded from, a community) combine to achieve the destruction of the individual" (21).

9. Jacques Derrida, "Structure, Sign, and Play in the Discourse of the
Human Sciences," 279.

10. Safaa Fathy, "Marrane, figure en ruine," 145.

11. For a different take on exemplarity in this *novela*, intelligently setting
out the limits of the pedagogical, casuistic interpretation of "El licenciado
Vidriera," see Ruth Fine, "La reescritura cervantina de la literatura sapiencial
en 'El licenciado Vidriera' y 'El rufián dichoso.'" For a more conventional
account of humanistic-pedagogical exemplarity in the *novelas*, see Stanislav
Zimic, *De esto y aquello en las obras de Cervantes*, in particular 247–48, and the
suggestion that the source for the *novelas* (or for their problematic) lies in the
Colloquies of Erasmus.

12. Fathy and Derrida, *Tourner les mots*, 133.

13. Sebastián de Covarrubias, *Tesoro de la lengua Castellana, o española*.

WORKS CITED

Bielik-Robson, Agata. *Jewish Cryptotheologies of Late Modernity: Philosophical Marranos*. New York: Routledge, 2014.

Cervantes, Miguel de. *The Exemplary Novels of Miguel de Cervantes Saavedra*. Translated by Walter K. Kelly. London: H. H. Bohn, 1855.

———. *Novelas Ejemplares*. Edited by Jorge García López. Madrid: Real Academia Española, 2013.

———. *Six Exemplary Novels*. Translated by Harriet de Onís. Woodbury, N.Y.: Barron's, 1961.

Clamurro, William H. "Hacia una lectura ideológica de las *Novelas ejemplares*: El caso de 'El licenciado Vidriera.'" In *Cervantes y su mundo*, edited by Eva Reichenberger, 6:19–38. Kasser: Reichenberger, 2004–10.

Covarrubias, Sebastián de. *Tesoro de la lengua Castellana, o española*. Madrid: Luis Sánchez, 1611.

Derrida, Jacques. *Paper Machine*. Translated by Rachel Bowlby. Stanford: Stanford University Press, 2005.

———. "Structure, Sign, and Play in the Discourse of the Human Sciences." In Jacques Derrida, *Writing and Difference*, translated by Alan Bass. London: Routledge, 1978.

Fathy, Safaa. "Marrane, figure en ruine." In *Tourner les mots: Au bord d'un film*, by Jacques Derrida and Safaa Fathy. Paris: Galilée, 2000.

Fathy, Safaa, and Jacques Derrida. *D'ailleurs, Derrida*. A film (1 hr., 8 min.) featuring Jacques Derrida. Montparnasse, 1999. Reissued 2008, DVD, including *Nom à la mer*, a film by Safaa Fathy with Jacques Derrida (29 min.); *De tout coeur*, a film by Safaa Fathy with Jacques Derrida (54 min.).

Fine, Ruth. "La reescritura cervantina de la literatura sapiencial en 'El licenciado Vidriera' y 'El rufián dichoso.'" In *Cervantes en la modernidad*, edited by José Ángel Ascunce and Alberto Rodríguez, 103–23. Kassel: Reichenberger, 2008.

Foster, Ricardo. "La ficción marrana: claves para una historia a contrapelo de la subjetividad moderna." In *Crítica y sospecha*. Buenos Aires: Paidós, 2003.

Gil-Osle, Juan Pablo. *Amistades imperfectas: Del humanismo a la ilustración con Cervantes*. Madrid: Iberoamericana, 2013.

Goldschmit, Marc. *L'hypothèse du Marrane: Le théâtre judéo-chrétien de la pensée plitique*. Paris: du Félin, 2014.

Graff Zivin, Erin. "Aporias of Marranismo: Sabina Berman's *En el nombre de Dios* and Jom Tob Azulay's *O Judeu*." *CR: The New Centennial Review* 12, no. 3 (2012): 187–216.

———. *Figurative Inquisitions: Conversion, Torture, and Truth in the Luso-Hispanic Atlantic*. Evanston, Ill.: Northwestern University Press, 2014.

————. "Politics against Ethics." *Política Común* 4 (2013), http://quod.lib
.umich.edu/p/pc.

Hamacher, Werner. *Minima Philologica*. Translated by Catharine Diehl and
Jason Groves. New York: Fordham University Press, 2015.

Kamuf, Peggy. *To Follow: The Wake of Jacques Derrida*. Edinburgh: Edinburgh
University Press, 2010.

Kleinberg, Ethan. "Not Yet Marrano: Levinas, Derrida, and the Ontology of
Being Jewish." In *The Trace of God: Derrida and Religion*, edited by Edward
Baring and Peter E. Gordon, 39–58. New York: Fordham University
Press, 2014.

Leibovici, Martine. "Jacques Derrida au site de 'l'entre': Identification
marrane et anamnèse autobiographique." *Rue Descartes* 81, no. 2 (2014):
102–15.

Lezra, Jacques. "The Disciplining of don Quijote and the Discipline of
Literary Studies." *eHumanista/Cervantes* 1 (2012): 488–513, http://www
.ehumanista.ucsb.edu/Cervantes/volume%201/index.shtml.

————. "Marranes que nous sommes?" *Rue Descartes* 66, no. 2 (2009): 44–57.

Molho, Mauricio. "Una dama de todo rumbo y manejo: para una lectura de
'El licenciado Vidriera.'" In *Erotismo en las letras hispánicas: Aspectos, modos
y fronteras*, edited by Luce López-Baralt and Francisco Márquez Villa-
nueva, 387–406. México: El Colegio de México, 1995.

Moreiras, Alberto. "Common Political Democracy: The Marrano Register."
In *Impasses of the Post-Global: Theory in the Era of Climate Change*, edited by
Henry Sussman, 2:175–93. Ann Arbor: University of Michigan Libraries,
www.openhumanitiespress.org, 2012.

————. *Línea de sombra: El no sujeto de lo político*. Santiago de Chile: Palinodia,
2006.

Pérez de Leon, Vicente. *Cervantes y el Cuarto misterio*. Alcalá de Henares:
Centro de Estudios Cervantinos, 2010.

Ruan, Felipe. "Carta de guía, carto-grafía: Fallas y fisuras en 'El licenciado
Vidriera.'" *Cervantes* 20, no. 2 (2000): 151–62.

Zimic, Stanislav. *De esto y aquello en las obras de Cervantes*. Newark, Del.: Juan
de la Cuesta-Hispanic Monographs, 2010.

CHAPTER 2

Spectral Comparisons: Cortázar and Derrida

David Kelman

¿Cómo decir en español: *haunted*?
[How to say *haunted* in Spanish?]

—JULIO CORTÁZAR, *Imagen de John Keats*

Someone, a comparatist by training, walks into a comparative literature conference and says: "I want monolingualism to teach me how to compare." This might sound like the beginning of a joke, since it asserts (or demands) that one could learn how to compare literatures in different languages by focusing on only one language. This could only be a joke, even if it's not a particularly funny one. After all, how would it be possible to think together the study of delimited linguistic areas (for example, Hispanism) and the comparative study of an area without limits ("the world")? At stake here is not the set of protocols that organize academic disciplines but rather the notion of sovereignty that conditions these disciplines. Although both comparative literature and the monolingual disciplines rely on the same principle of sovereignty (the power to decide between the norm and what threatens the norm), it is also true that these disciplines exercise their sovereignty in different ways. For instance, the monolingual disciplines traditionally decide on what belongs and what does not belong to a field by policing the boundaries of linguistic areas (Hispanism, Francophonie, English studies, etc.), whereas comparative literature traditionally takes a more panoptic approach, deciding on the proper or legitimate relation between multiple linguistic areas in order to constitute a "world" or a "world literature."[1] Nevertheless, to think together these two paradigms of disciplinary sovereignty would not only highlight the way these disciplines organize themselves but would also challenge the notion of sovereignty that makes these disciplines possible.

In what follows I would like to open up this question of disciplinary sovereignty by thinking together "monolingualism" and "comparative literature," that is, to think together the limit and the unlimited. But what could a comparatist possibly learn from a focus that attends to only one language at a time? In a sense, there seems to be an obvious response to this question, as if there really were no debate here. After all, comparative literature is nothing without a strict focus on one text in one language at a time. Comparative literature needs the discreteness of national literatures and the regional context for comparison to work: There must be difference in order to compare. The point now, however, is not to move from one limited context to another and then compare the differences, but rather to think together the limited and the unlimited, to think *at the same time* the limited and the unlimited. In other words, the idea is not simply to expand the limits of comparative literature so that other contexts are made more visible, but rather to read that which is not present (the outside, the "world") within the limited context of the "monolingual."[2] It turns out, in fact, that any attempt to think together "comparative literature" and "monolingualism" inevitably forces a new understanding of the effects of the limit.

This question of the limit comes up in a surprising way in the works of two very different writers: Julio Cortázar and Jacques Derrida.[3] Although these two writers are often worlds apart, nevertheless I argue that there is something of a long-distance communication between them. In fact, one way they communicate is around this question of communication, especially the way they both try to think through a theory of communication without communication, a theory of relation without relation, and perhaps even a theory of comparison without comparison. By bringing together these two writers around the question of limited and unlimited communication, I would like to imagine a comparison that takes place *beyond visibility*: a spectral or ghostly comparison. At the same time, this "new" comparative literature would open up a thinking of disciplinary sovereignty that is not based on the distinction between visibility and invisibility. This comparative literature would be "new" in the sense that it has never been seen before (and perhaps never will), since it emerges from a sovereignty based on the ghost or the phantasm.

Dealing with Ghosts

Before asking how a certain "monolingualism" could open up a comparative literature to come, it would first be necessary to address how I am using the word "monolingualism" here. For instance, it would seem that one should be able to distinguish between monolingualism as a cultural norm and monolingualism as a condition of academic studies (Hispanism, English studies, Francophonie, etc.). As a cultural norm, monolingualism has been a concern for those seeking to resist a contemporary political climate that is paradoxically both global and "English." To take one example among many, in April 2011 the executive council of the Modern Language Association (MLA) called for a new emphasis on advanced fluency in a nonnative language, explaining that "American monolingualism is an impediment to effective participation in a multilingual world" (*Learning Another Language: Goals and Challenges*). As a cultural norm, "American monolingualism" is a force that clearly threatens the vitality of a multilingual world that, at best, could resist the global paradigm of "English-only." In fact, Russell Berman, president of MLA in 2012, insists that monolingualism is not only threatening multilingualism, but also threatens the very vitality of the native tongue. He writes that "the lack of second-language learning is now spilling over into first-language literacy deficiencies. For all of our monolingualism, we don't even learn our one privileged language well" (Berman, "Real Language Crisis," 33). Monolingualism, as a cultural norm, is a self-defeating practice, since the very autonomy of monolingualism is also that which causes its own decay: The fullness of monolingualism is also its very deficiency.

It might seem that monolingualism as the condition of an academic discipline would be a different story. After all, most academic fields that focus on one language are precisely on the front line of a battle against cultural monolingualism. For instance, Hispanism in American universities would help combat the emphasis on "English only" in U.S. communities. But the same cannot be said about U.S. English studies, which for the most part stays bound to varieties of English in the United States, Britain, and the "world."[4] Nevertheless, even Hispanic studies, to continue with this example, remains precisely limited to Spanish (and not French, and not Nahuatl, and not Catalan, etc.). Although it is true that PhD programs in Spanish encourage or sometimes even require reading knowledge of another language (other than English and Spanish), this multilingual requirement is often framed within the wider hegemony of Spanish within the discipline of Hispanism.[5] As a monolinguistic discipline, Hispanism should police its own borders, even if exceptions to the rule are allowed precisely in order to contain and control that which goes beyond the realm of Hispanism proper. This policing task is the proper role of the sovereign, who must decide "whether there is an extreme emergency as well as what must be done to eliminate it" (Schmitt, *Political Theology*, 7). Hispanism, as a monolinguistic academic discourse, is obliged to eliminate that which goes beyond linguistic norms, whether through rigorous exclusion or through strategies of containment. The very rigor of Hispanism is that it constitutes itself as an autonomous discipline that must protect itself from every foreign force that threatens to emerge from the outside.

There is nothing new in these observations, but the banality of this description should not hide the fact that academic monolingualism can indeed fall into the same problems that beset monolingualism as a cultural norm. At the very least, it is indeed possible to speak of a generalized monolingualism that would include the monolinguistic academic disciplines. Jacques Derrida brings out the paradoxical structure of monolingualism in his short book *Monolingualism of the Other*. For Derrida, monolingualism is simply unavoidable: To speak at all is to dwell in monolingualism and to allow monolingualism to dwell in me. Monolingualism is indisputable, since "I cannot challenge it except by testifying to its omnipresence in me. It would always have preceded me. It is me. For me, this monolingualism is me. . . . It constitutes me, it dictates even the ipseity of all things to me" (1). In other words, I am autonomous precisely to the extent that I am monolingual: My (single) language constitutes my self, my "me." For that reason Derrida admits that the experience of monolingualism "would be ostensibly *autonomous*, because I have to speak this law [of language and law as language] and appropriate it in order to understand it *as if* I was giving it to myself," that is, as if engaging in the sovereign act of giving myself my own law (as if I were precisely auto-nomous). And yet monolingualism, he goes on to say, "remains necessarily *heteronomous*," since "I have only one language and it is not mine; my 'own' language is, for me, a language that cannot be assimilated. My language, the only one I hear myself speak and agree to speak, is the language of the other" (39, 25). Precisely in that experience of appropriating my own language, I am deprived of this language, since it always comes from the other, from somewhere else outside myself. Monolingualism is therefore the experience of autonomy and sovereignty, but at the same time it is the experience of being utterly deprived of, or precisely alienated from my language.

And yet this alienation is not an accidental deprivation or "deficiency," but rather a constitutive "lack." Here Derrida speaks of a structure of alienation without alienation: "This abiding 'alienation' [*aliénation à de-meure*] appears, like 'lack,' to be constitutive. But it is neither a lack nor an alienation; it lacks nothing that precedes or follows it, it alienates no *ipseity*, no property, and no self that has ever been able to represent its watchful eye" (25). Monolingualism constitutes my *ipseity* in such a way that it de-prives me of any ipseity, of any autonomy: it is an ipseity without ipseity and an alienation without alienation. For that reason Derrida explains that this experience of monolingualism is also the experience of the phantasm, or an autonomous appearing without appearance:

> This structure of alienation without alienation, this inalienable alien-ation, is not only the origin of our responsibility, it also structures the peculiarity [*le propre*] and property of language. It institutes the *phe-nomenon* of hearing-oneself-speak in order to mean-to-say [*pour vouloir dire*]. But here, we must say the *phenomenon* as *phantasm*. Let us refer for the moment to the semantic and etymological affinity that associates the phantasm to the *phainesthai*, to phenomenality, but also the spec-trality of the phenomenon. *Phantasma* is also the phantom, the double, or the ghost. (25)

The experience of monolingualism is therefore the experience of the phan-tasm: The mere act of speaking not only evokes the seemingly autonomous experience of hearing oneself speak but also conjures up the ghost of the other speaking "in me." Paradoxically, then, monolingualism is autono-mous only insofar as it presents itself in the mode of the fantastic: It ap-pears phantasmatically as something that always comes (back) from the inapparent other.

To deal with monolingualism is therefore already to conjure up the phantasm. And yet it is also clear that monolingualism is often used to conjure away or exorcise specters. As Derrida notes in *Specters of Marx*, "There has *never* been a scholar who really, and as scholar, deals with ghosts" (Derrida, *Specters*, 11, my emphasis). At best, Derrida awaits the arrival of a scholar who would be able to speak a monolingualism *of* the other, that is, a monolingualism that belongs to the other. He therefore opens up the possibility of a scholarship that not only would be able to ad-dress a ghost (*fantôme*), but would, in the very discourse of this scholarship, open itself up to invasions of the phantasm or the fantastic other (Derrida, *Specters*, 33).

To be fair, it is not simply a question of choosing which kind of scholar one would like to be, as if one could simply choose to be a scholar who deals with ghosts, or as if one could choose to invite the invasion of the phantasm into one's own scholarship. It is a not a question of choice, in part because it has to do with protocols specific to scholarship. How can a scholar, who by definition limits himself or herself to a certain field (linguistic, historical, generic, etc.) bear witness to that which does not present itself as such? How can a scholar, who by definition must abide by strict definitions, bear witness to that which does not remain bound within definitions? In short, how can a scholar bear witness to that which has no presence and therefore cannot be mobilized precisely as evidence? A legitimate scholar, Derrida reminds us in *Specters of Marx*, must "believe in the sharp distinction between the real and the unreal, the actual and the inactual, the living and the non-living, being and non-being . . . , in the opposition between what is present and what is not" (11). In other words, a legitimate scholar could not simply choose to remain monolingual while also insisting or promising a comparative perspective, since this stance would in effect give up the role of scholar, that is, the one who presents a real distinction between what is there and what is not.

In an essay from 1979, "Living On / Border Lines," Derrida gives a concrete example of a kind of scholarship that *cannot* be performed, a fantastic or phantasmic scholarship, a scholarship that deals with ghosts. This kind of scholarship is illegitimate precisely to the extent that it seeks (or pretends) to bear witness to what is not present. He speaks of a scene of teaching that involves something of a spectral comparison between Percy Bysshe Shelley and Maurice Blanchot: "You can't give a course on Shelley without ever mentioning him, pretending to deal with Blanchot, and more than a few others" (Derrida, "Living," 84). Derrida admits that this scenario would go against the reading protocols of legitimate scholarship; it would be quite simply an illegitimate educational operation ("Opération illégitime dans l'enseignement") (*Parages*, 128). He writes: "This operation would never be considered legitimate on the part of a teacher, who must give his references and tell what he's talking about, giving it a recognizable title" ("Living," 84). The scene of teaching, after all, depends precisely on presentation: The teacher must present a text, must refer to what is evident (as evidence), and must refer to it in a proper way (calling the text by its proper name and not by a code name or allegorical title). Without this emphasis on presence, there is precisely nothing (evident) to teach and nothing (evident) to learn.

Furthermore, this attempt to teach Shelley by presenting only Blanchot runs into larger problems concerning the notion of the limit or border, here the border between two texts. After all, the illegitimate operation of reading Shelley by focusing only on Blanchot transgresses normative laws of border control, since a "text," normatively conceived, would be defined by clearly demarcated borders, and in fact would be constituted by a very strict delimitation. Derrida asks: "How can one text, assuming its unity, give or present another to be read, without touching it, without saying anything about it, practically without referring to it?" ("Living," 80). This seems to be a rhetorical question, because the answer is clear: You simply cannot operate this way (according to normative protocols, such as the assumption of a text's unity). The American Comparative Literature Association's 1975 report on the discipline warned explicitly about the specter of "invisible comparisons" and worries about the "relaxing of discipline" that this kind of comparison would entail (Greene, "Greene Report," 36). Derrida likewise notes that the illegitimacy of invisible comparisons stems from the way they work against the norms of readability, that is, the law of readable relations: "And your transitions have to be readable, that is, in accordance with criteria of readability very firmly established, and long since" ("Living," 85). In other words, relations between texts must not only be readable, but must be readable according to long-established norms of readability. It would therefore seem bizarre, or illegitimate, to ask mono-lingualism to help theorize a comparative literature to come, that is, a comparative literature that does not use long-established norms in order to make connections (Derrida writes: "Et il faut enchaîner lisiblement [and it's necessary to make legible connections]"), a comparative literature that upends those norms precisely by making connections with ghosts or by inviting the phantasm into scholarship (Derrida, *Parages*, 128). A "mono-linguistic" comparative literature would seem dangerously close to this kind of invisible or spectral comparison. Imagine a scholar arriving at an academic conference, announcing that monolingualism could teach us to perform spectral comparisons. Laughter (or worse) could be the only re-sponse: "It's enough to make a philologist laugh (or scream)" (Derrida, "Living," 147).

And yet what if this joke, which would like to think together mono-lingualism and comparative literature, could be entertained in some way? What would comparative literature look like if it remained within strict limits (for instance, the limits of Spanish), and yet at the same time com-municated with something that is not present? As Derrida suggests, mono-lingualism is always beholden to the other, even if specific instances of monolingualism insist on annihilating the other, or reducing the other to the same, which would have the same effect. What if a new comparativ-ism could address the ghostly other of monolingualism without, however, forcing this other into visibility? How might a certain monolingualism—

Hispanism, for example—help us imagine a comparative literature that operates beyond the distinction between the visible and the invisible, beyond the distinction between presence and absence? What would this "spectral comparison" look like?

Spectral Comparisons

Surprisingly, a model of spectral comparisons emerges from a lecture on the genre of the short story, given by Julio Cortázar in Cuba in 1963. In Cortázar's hands, the short story (or *cuento*) presents an autonomous structure that nevertheless communicates with something beyond itself and receives communications from this "beyond." Even though Cortázar's lecture, "Algunos aspectos del cuento" ("Some Aspects of the Short Story"), refers explicitly to the literary form of the short story, his term "*cuento*" plays out in a larger semantic realm than the term "short story" in English. For Cortázar, the cuento is a more general structure of "communication," taking that word not only in the sense of sending and receiving messages, but also and more generally in the sense of a passage or relay (as when we say that one room communicates with another). I turn to this lecture in order to bring out Cortázar's idiosyncratic theorization of the cuento as a communicative structure that never presents this communication as such, a structure that presents a passageway to the outside without ever presenting that outside. Cortázar's theory of the cuento therefore offers a way to think about a comparison without comparison, a way to imagine, in the mode of a cuento, a spectral comparison.

A discourse or communication about the Hispanic cuento comes up as an opportunity—but also as a problem—throughout Cortázar's lecture. On the one hand, he sees the present moment (Cuba, 1963) as a great opportunity. He writes: "The opportunity to exchange ideas about the short story interests me for various reasons" (Cortázar, "Algunos," 369).[6] What interests Cortázar, in other words, is not simply lecturing about the cuento, but precisely this opportunity to exchange ideas ("La oportunidad de cambiar ideas") about this form. He embraces this opportunity to produce a communication, in Spanish, on the form of the cuento. The most important reason for embracing this exchange of ideas about the cuento is that, in some sense, the communication or conversation has already started, or should have already started, for "us." He states: "A discussion of the short story should interest us especially, since almost all the Spanish-speaking countries of America give the story great importance, which it has never had in other Latin countries like France or Spain" (Cortázar, "Some," 245).

Cortázar is not interested in establishing what he calls a "Latin" discourse (since that would include France and Spain, among others), and he is not interested in a Latin American discourse (since that would include Brazil, the French Caribbean, etc.). Rather, he would like to set up strict limits: He would like to study the Hispanic cuento in the Americas, the cuento in "los países americanos de lengua española" (Cortázar, "Algunos," 369). There is a strict monolingual context that is already giving attention to this form, and it is therefore time to seize this opportunity to theorize this form. Cortázar's "Hispanism" founds itself on this new opportunity.

However, this opportunity is also a problem, since the limits that make possible a monolingual communication about the cuento have also cut short this communication. Cortázar explains: "In America, in Cuba, just as in Mexico or Chile or Argentina, a great number of short-story writers worked from the beginning of this century on, without knowing each other, discovering each other almost posthumously" (Cortázar, "Some," 246). Within this delimited communicative context ("los países americanos de lengua española," which are here exemplified by Cuba, Mexico, Chile, and Argentina) a communication problem arises. The problem is not that writers are ignoring the cuento. On the contrary, they are focusing on it with unprecedented intensity, without, however, talking about it, without communicating about it among themselves, and most of all without recognizing each other, "sin conocerse mucho entre sí" (Cortázar, "Algunos," 370). It is as if the limits that would make possible the monolinguistic study of the cuento (among "los países americanos de lengua española") have multiplied, interrupting *any* line of communication. It therefore seems that, on the one hand, there is already a subject, a "we" or "us" ("hablar del cuento tiene un interés especial para nosotros") that is talking or has been talking about the cuento, giving this genre an exceptional significance ("una importancia excepcional"), and therefore "we" need only seize this opportunity to have a conversation that in some sense has already started (369). But on the other hand, this conversation about the cuento is not passing easily through national or geographical borders: The attention to the cuento in one country or region is not communicating with another country or region. Even when this conversation does manage to get transmitted across boundaries or limits, there is nevertheless a crucial delay that marks that passage. The passage through the boundary produces a passing away (discovery happens in an almost posthumous way, he says, "de manera casi póstuma"), thus suggesting that there are no actualized connections between the various countries (370). Cortázar would therefore like to address not only an opportunity but also a problem: It is the threat that the study of the Hispanic cuento could end up, from the beginning, a posthumous affair, or a dialogue among ghosts. A study of the monolingual cuento, then, is far from an obvious or evident fact. It is beset by the problems of an internal comparativism that threatens it from the beginning, since the grounds for comparison (relation, or communication as relation) might fail to materialize, thus turning the act of comparing one cuento with another into a posthumous affair, an exchange of ghosts.

This becoming-posthumous hangs over Cortázar's lecture as a constant menace, even as it represents perhaps the only possible conditions for a "communication." In fact, the scene of address, inscribed in Cortázar's lecture, begins with the threat of disappearance, or more precisely, with the appearance of a ghost or specter. In what follows, Cortázar precisely presents himself as a nonpresence:

> I find myself before you in something of a paradoxical situation. An Argentine short-story writer is here to exchange ideas about the short story, without his audience knowing anything about his work, with a few exceptions. The cultural isolation that continues to be so detrimental to our two countries, combined with the unjust isolation [*la injusta incomunicación*] that has been imposed on Cuba today, have determined that my books, which are already quite a few, have only rarely found their way to such an enthusiastic audience as yourselves. The worst of this is not so much that you have not had the opportunity to judge my short stories, but that I feel something like a ghost [*fantasma*] coming before you today, since I don't have the confidence that accompanies writers when they know that their work, produced over many years, has preceded them. (367)

The short-story writer appears "here" without appearing; he just finds himself here ("Me encuentro"), almost as surprised as anyone else by this sudden appearance. After all, he is speaking to his audience in an age of "la injusta incomunicación" or unjust isolation, a contemporary period that is politically marked by a lack of communication and connection. Certainly this "injusta incomunicación" describes Cuba's political situation in 1963, but, as noted earlier, it also conditions all communication between Spanish-speaking countries. Cortázar therefore finds it paradoxical that he is now present in Cuba, about to communicate his present voice to his present audience, because at the same time he is somehow not there, because of this age of "la injusta incomunicación." Thus, even given this actualized presence, he nevertheless finds that there is nothing *given* about the situation: He feels like a ghost, "como un fantasma," who has come to speak to his interlocutors (367). Like Hamlet's father, Cortázar is the ghost who comes to speak to a specific audience, "un fantasma que viene a hablarles," but unlike Hamlet's father, the Argentine writer finds that the labor of his works does not precede him: He appears "without the relative tranquility that accompanies writers when they know that their work, produced over many years, has preceded them [sin esa relativa tranquilidad que da siempre el saberse precedido por la labor cumplida a lo largo de los años]" (367). In other words, Cortázar's apparition is quite literally unprecedented: No one was waiting for his arrival; he was unanticipated, unhoped for, unexpected. For that reason, Cortázar notes that his appearance is plagued by a spectral quality ("calidad espectral"), which is here associated with the threat of disappearance (367). In fact, he jokes (but is he joking?) that he wouldn't be surprised if he should suddenly disappear in the middle of a sentence: "Si de golpe desaparezco en mitad de una frase, no me sorprenderé demasiado" (367). This threat of disappearance, or rather appearance as the threat of disappearance, is precisely what hangs over his entire discourse; that is, it haunts his *Hispanic* discourse in the age of "la injusta incomunicación." Cortázar's Hispanism thus founds itself not only on the opportunity to theorize the Spanish American cuento, but also on the inability to take advantage of the opportunity to constitute this Hispanic discourse, due to the threat of the *fantasma*. Even when communication takes place (as this lecture in Cuba seems to demonstrate), there is still an *incomunicación* that threatens the very appearance of that discourse. An unjust lack of communication and connection between Hispanic countries ends up producing a constant interruption of communication, even when communication seems most successful. This communication without communication is what Cortázar calls "el fantasma": The ghost happens whenever discourse is internally threatened by "la injusta incomunicación."

"Incommunication" (which we could define as a lack of communication or connection even at the moment of "successful" communication) is therefore not an accidental occurrence, a problem that happens only in the world of diplomacy and policy, but rather becomes a material condition of this Hispanic discourse. Even when communication is indeed taking place (for instance, when speaking in Spanish with his Cuban audience about the study of the Hispanic cuento), the condition of "incommunication" turns this act of communication into a discourse of the *fantasma*, a fantastic discourse. In any case, this is the cuento that Cortázar tells his audience about the problems and opportunities that arise when one tries to communicate in the age of incommunication. In fact, this is the kind of cuento he always tells, a type of cuento that he links precisely to the "fantastic."

Almost all the stories I have written belong to the genre known as
"fantastic" for lack of a better term, and they are opposed to that false
realism which consists of believing that everything can be described
and explained as it was accepted by the scientific and philosophical
optimism of the eighteenth century; that is, within a world directed
more or less harmoniously by a system of laws, principles, cause-and-
effect relations, defined psychologies, and well-mapped geographies. In
my case, the suspicion of another order, more secret and less communicable, and the rich discovery of Alfred Jarry, for whom the true study of
reality lay not in its laws, but in the exceptions to those laws, have been
some of the orienting principles of my personal search for a literature
beyond all ingenuous realism. (Cortázar, "Some," 245)

The fantastic, for Cortázar, is not a specific theme, but rather corresponds
to a movement beyond well-defined limits or boundaries. His notion of the
fantastic focuses not on the laws or limits of reality but on the exceptions
to those laws or limits ("no . . . en las leyes sino en las excepciones a esas
leyes" ["Algunos," 368]). The fantastic emerges, then, precisely as a state of
exception, and the function of the fantastic story would seem to be to communicate with this outside, to establish a séance, as it were, with the other
side. But of course this state of exception is also touched by an irreducible incommunication, since the fantastic always involves a relation with
an outside that is less communicable, or at least involves the suspicion of
an order that is less communicable (secret) and therefore "other" ("la sospecha de otro orden más secreto y menos comunicable") (368). If the fantastic communicates with the outside, this "outside" is not the domain of
transparency and illumination (it would be outside "a system of laws, principles, cause-and-effect relations, defined psychologies, and well-mapped
geographies"). Rather, the fantastic only "appears" as a resistance to the
demand for what Derrida calls "absolute phenomenality" (Derrida, *Without Alibi*, 63); the fantastic emerges as a resistance to well-defined borders,
boundaries, and limits that would circumscribe something clearly visible.
The fantastic would therefore have an aphenomenal or avisual appearance,
if these terms are understood as a resistance to absolute phenomenality and
not in opposition to the phenomenal or the visual: It is a phenomenality
that deals with the phantasm. And this is the cuento that Cortázar always
tells: On the one hand, it is a discourse of the fantastic that communicates
beyond certain limits, but on the other hand, this communication is "más
secreto y menos comunicable": It does not quite appear (it remains secret)
and it is not quite communicable.

Although it is true that Cortázar goes on to say that not all cuentos are fantastic, nevertheless his theory of the cuento ends up suggesting that this genre is generally phantasmic, that is, it has a spectral or not-quite-phenomenal quality to it. He begins, again, with the notion of the limit: Whereas the novel has no limits, he insists that "the short story begins with the notion of limits" ("el cuento parte de la noción del límite") (Cortázar, "Some," 246; "Algunos," 371). The point for Cortázar is not simply that the cuento happens to be short or brief, but rather that its condition of possibility is the *limit*. Whereas the novel extends itself, develops itself, exhausts its material, the cuento withdraws from communication and places determined limits on its communicative capacity, that is, on its ability to develop itself on the page, connect with other ideas, associate with other words: It is closed to the outside.[7] In a well-known analogy, Cortázar compares the cuento to the photograph, noting that both forms are constituted not only by this notion of the limit, but also, strangely, the breaking of that limit or boundary:

> The photographer or the story writer finds himself obliged to choose and delimit an image or an event which must be meaningful, which is meaningful not only in itself, but rather is capable of acting on the viewer or the reader as a kind of opening, an impetus which projects the intelligence and the sensibility toward something which goes well beyond the visual or literary anecdote contained in the photograph or the story. ("Some," 247)

At first this operation would seem to imply that the cuento is indeed a successful communicative device: A cuento produces a transmission whereby the form of the story sets up a line of communication between the event narrated and something outside of that event. However, despite the visual metaphor implied by the visible comparison to photography, the cuento projects the sensibility toward something nonsensory, something that precisely goes well beyond (*mucho más allá de*) what can be seen (an image) or narrated (an anecdote), that is, beyond what can be "contained" within a photograph or story ("Algunos," 372). This "beyond" takes us not only beyond determined limits but rather beyond appearance. While the cuento indeed stays focused on an event (*acaecimiento*, what befalls), this structure is nevertheless haunted by an event that never quite takes place or occurs, that never really appears, since it goes beyond the frame of the phenomenal. Cortázar uses this phenomenal comparison (he visibly compares the cuento and the photograph) in order to suggest an operation or movement that conjures up the nonpresentable, the nonphenomenal. The cuento (or the photograph) is constituted by the notion of the limit, but this now means that even when a communication or connection is made with the outside, this outside-the-frame remains essentially "más secreto y menos comunicable": a phantasmic discourse.

Cortázar's lecture therefore provides a model of comparison without comparison, that is, a structure that focuses on only one event at a time while also allowing another event to take place without appearance. Indeed, Cortázar seems to invite a way to think about a "comparative literature" within Hispanic studies, but it would be a ghostly comparative literature or not-quite-perceptual comparative literature that emerges from the strictest monolingualism.[8] This kind of spectral comparison would not be fully compared by the Hispanist or even by the comparatist, since a ghostly distance would intervene at every moment. Comparison as such never takes place, but a ghostly comparison nevertheless becomes operational within the structure of the cuento. Curiously, however, a scholar cannot come along and choose this mode of comparison, as if spectral comparisons were one mode among many within the comparatist's toolbox. On the contrary, the structure of the cuento necessitates a new thinking of the sovereignty of the scholar. Although the Hispanist in the age of unjust incommunication can focus only on a delimited text or event, this limited focus is never fully under the control of the scholar, since the limited text is always opening itself up to an outside that cannot be claimed or possessed. For this reason Cortázar admits that his own cuentos were written without intention, as if an outside force were controlling his will: "In my case, the great majority of my stories were written outside my will, above or below my conscious reasoning, as if I were no more than a medium through which an alien force passed and took shape" ("Some," 248). Cortázar makes it clear that his cuentos are determined by a figure or force that goes beyond the visible and the intentional, "al margen de mi voluntad," on the margins of his will or beyond his control ("Algunos," 374). This marginal figure is not an image that the text refers or alludes to, but is rather an alien force, "una fuerza ajena," a sovereignty or might that stands outside the cuento and yet determines it in an indeterminable or unforeseeable way (374). This "force" has the sovereignty of whatever appears without appearing; its force applies pressure without fully belonging (the force is *ajena*). This sovereign figure is an essentially avisual force that constitutes the cuento, and yet this alien force has no place in the cuento. It does not appear in the cuento, and the writer of the cuento has no control over it: The sovereign figure takes place without taking (a) place. For that reason Cortázar can say that the cuento is essentially written outside of his control ("al margen de mi voluntad"). However, this is not something that simply happens in the "majority" of his cuentos, but rather stands as a structural principle of the cuento: The cuento is not a cuento (it is not *significant*) unless there is this outside force that breaks the very limits of the cuento ("Un cuento es significativo cuando quiebra sus propios límites" [Cortázar, "Algunos," 373]). The sovereign force is both outside ("ajena") and inside the cuento, in the sense that a cuento cannot take place unless there is this breach of limits.

Strangely, then, the cuento models a notion of sovereignty that is precisely divisible, an apparent paradox since sovereignty makes sense only if it is indivisible and unified: The sovereign by definition is the first and last word.[9] On the one hand, the cuento, because of its "spherical" form, seems closed off to the outside and therefore seems to retain absolute autonomy; and yet on the other hand, the cuento is constituted by an alien force that is nevertheless "inside" this discursive structure. The Hispanist seems to have complete control over his or her own domain (within determined limits), and yet everything within these limits is determined *secretly* by *una fuerza ajena*, a sovereign figure that does not belong. At the same time, because this Hispanic discourse becomes significant only when it opens up unintentionally to something outside of its limits, the Hispanist ends up producing a relation without relation with what lies outside the frame. It is precisely for this reason that this form (the cuento, the Hispanist discourse) can stand as the very model of an aphenomenal, avisual, and otherwise-than-sovereign comparative literature: It institutes a discourse that limits itself within determined boundaries and yet also remains tied to what lies outside those determined limits. The task of this spectral comparative literature would be to practice an unconditional yet divisible Humanities, one that "thinks *in* the Humanities the irreducibility of their outside and of their future" (Derrida, *Without Alibi*, 236). A comparative literature within Hispanism (a spectral comparison) would entail a limited focus on only one language at a time but would at the same time open itself to the outside so that this one language, this one literature, would be touched by an alien force. This would be the task of a spectral comparative literature, a delimited monolingualism that is haunted by what lies beyond its own limits.

NOTES

1. On comparative literature's pretensions to the "world," see Ferris's "Indiscipline," as well as Derrida's "Who or What Is Compared?" See

Kelman, "Comparative Literature in the Age of the Great Telematic Network," for a discussion of an internal resistance to this totalizing tendency.

2. See *Comparative Cultural Criticism and Latin America* by Sophia A. McClennen and Earl E. Fitz, as well as Gayatri Chakravorty Spivak's *Death of a Discipline*, for attempts to reposition comparative studies around the Global South. Although these arguments can certainly be credited with a productive opening of comparative studies, they tend to rely on a strict difference between what is *inside* and *outside* the canon, without a corresponding attempt to touch the problem of limits and the notion of sovereignty that underlie these disciplinary moves.

3. I thank Matthew Berger for his conversations on Cortázar (during an independent study on theories of the short story he took with me in 2010) and Derrida (during his time as my research assistant on comparative literature in 2011–12).

4. The MLA Executive Council has recently proposed that doctoral programs in English should include proficiency in more than one foreign language, thus effectively linking the organization's stances on cultural monolingualism and its stances on academic (or disciplinary) monolingualism (*Statement on Language Requirements for Doctoral Programs in English*).

5. McClennen and Fitz explicitly recommend that Latin Americanists develop this emphasis on multiple languages (especially Portuguese, but also Dutch, French, and various indigenous languages, depending on the specialization), but of course this emphasis is always *limited* to a particular field of study. Although it is difficult to argue against these recommendations, one should still note the emphasis on disciplinary limits, that is, on what is "properly" inside this or that field within Latin American studies. This concern is of particular interest to theorists of Latin Americanism, precisely around the question of sovereignty. As Gareth Williams has noted, any attempt by the intellectual to expand the field of Latin American studies always brings with it the figure of the academic sovereign who *decides* and *legislates* the location of borders between the proper and the improper (Williams, "La deconstrucción y los estudios subalternos," 229).

6. All translations are my own except where noted. The published English translation of Cortázar's lecture, which I will use where noted, is highly edited, at times skipping whole paragraphs.

7. In the Berkeley lectures, Cortázar speaks of the cuento as "a strange closed order" and alludes to "the fact that the cuento has an internal, architectonic obligation to not remain open, but rather to close itself off like a sphere" (Cortázar, *Clases*, 31). See Brescia, Di Gerónimo, and Kelman ("Afterlife of Storytelling") for distinct developments of Cortázar's poetics of the short story.

8. Cf. Cathy Caruth's similar evocation of a bilingualism that emerges from monolingualism, "the possibility for a single language to become the site of its own 'comparison'" (Caruth, "Orphaned," 240).

9. As Derrida notes in *The Beast and the Sovereign I*, "A divisible sovereignty is no longer a sovereignty, a sovereignty worthy of the name, i.e. pure and unconditional" (Derrida, *Beast I*, 76–77). Of course, this thinking of a *divisible* sovereignty would enact a deconstruction of the traditional concept of sovereignty.

WORKS CITED

Berman, Russell A. "The Real Language Crisis." *Academe* 97, no. 5 (2011): 30–34.

Brescia, Pablo. *Modelos y prácticas en el cuento hispanoamericano: Arreola, Borges, Cortázar*. Madrid: Iberoamericana, 2011.

Caruth, Cathy. "Orphaned Language: Traumatic Crossings in Literature and History." In *A Companion to Comparative Literature*, edited by Ali Behdad and Dominic Thomas, 239–53. West Sussex, UK: Blackwell, 2011.

Cortázar, Julio. "Algunos aspectos del cuento." In *Obra crítica / 2*, edited by Jaime Alazraki, 365–85. Buenos Aires: Alfaguara, 1994.

———. *Clases de literatura: Berkeley, 1980*. Edited by Carles Álvarez Garriga. Buenos Aires: Alfaguara, 2013.

———. *Imagen de John Keats*. Buenos Aires: Alfaguara, 1996.

———. "Some Aspects of the Short Story." Translated by Aden W. Hayes. In *The New Short Story Theories*, edited by Charles E. May. Athens: Ohio University Press, 1994.

Derrida, Jacques. *The Beast and the Sovereign 1*. Translated by Geoffrey Bennington. Chicago: University of Chicago Press, 2009.

———. "Living On / Border Lines." In *Deconstruction and Criticism*, 75–176. New York: Continuum, 1979.

———. *Monolingualism of the Other, or The Prosthesis of Origin*. Translated by Patrick Mensah. Stanford: Stanford University Press, 1998.

———. *Parages*. Paris: Éditions Galilée, 1986.

———. *Spectres de Marx*. Paris: Éditions Galilée, 1993.

———. *Specters of Marx: The State of the Debt, the Work of Mourning, and the New International*. Translated by Peggy Kamuf. New York: Routledge, 1994.

———. "Who or What Is Compared? The Concept of Comparative Literature and the Theoretical Problems of Translation." Translated by Eric Prenowitz. *Discourse* 30, nos. 1 & 2 (2008): 22–53.

———. *Without Alibi.* Edited and translated by Peggy Kamuf. Stanford: Stanford University Press, 2002.

Di Jerónimo. *Narrar por knock-out: La poética del cuento de Julio Cortázar.* Buenos Aires: Simurg, 2004.

Ferris, David. "Indiscipline." In *Comparative Literature in the Age of Globalization,* edited by Haun Saussy, 78–99. Baltimore: Johns Hopkins University Press, 2006.

Greene, Thomas. "The Greene Report, 1975: A Report on Standards." In *Comparative Literature in the Age of Multiculturalism,* edited by Charles Bernheimer. Baltimore: John Hopkins University Press, 1995.

Kelman, David. "The Afterlife of Storytelling: Julio Cortázar's Reading of Walter Benjamin and Edgar Allan Poe." *Comparative Literature* 60, no. 3 (2008): 244–60.

———. "Comparative Literature in the Age of the Great Telematic Network." *CR: The New Centennial Review* 14, no. 3 (2014): 111–38.

McClennen, Sophia, and Earl Fitz. *Comparative Cultural Criticism and Latin America.* West Lafayette, IN: Purdue University Press, 2004.

MLA Executive Council. *Learning Another Language: Goals and Challenges.* Modern Language Association, April 2011. Web. June 19, 2015.

———. *Statement on Language Requirements for Doctoral Programs in English.* Modern Language Association, February 2012. Web. June 19, 2015.

Schmitt, Carl. *Political Theology: Four Chapters on the Concept of Sovereignty.* Translated by George Schwab. Chicago: University of Chicago Press, 1985.

Spivak, Gayatri Chakravorty. *Death of a Discipline.* New York: Columbia University Press, 2003.

Williams, Gareth. "La deconstrucción y los estudios subalternos, o una llave de tuerca en la línea de montaje latinoamericanista." In *Treinta años de estudios literarios/culturales latinoamericanistas en Estados Unidos. Memorias, testimonios, reflexiones críticas,* edited by Hernán Vidal, 221–56. Pittsburgh: Biblioteca de América, 2008.

CHAPTER 3

On Mondialatinization, or Saving the Name of the Latin

Jaime Hanneken

If Derrida's concept of *mondialatinization*[1] is of consequence to the future prospects of Latin Americanism, it is at least in part because the conceptualization of Latin America, practically since it came to be called that, has been nourished by a belief so fervent in the ineffable, exceptional quality of "Latin" history and place as to be considered religious. Religious, to be sure, because it is mobilized in the name of the geographic, racial, and linguistic vicissitudes of Latinity, but more pointedly in the way this mobilization seeks salvation and self-preservation simultaneously in the purported singularity of Latin events, texts, cultures, and places, and in their untrammeled universalization. Thus, the name "Latin" serves Latin Americanism as a toponym for the same kind of autoimmune activity that Derrida sees patent in religion's mondialatinization.

As an intellectual aegis of culture and knowledge, recourse to Latin identity has traditionally been as empty as it is powerful. For early twentieth-century movements such as *Arielismo*, *Ateneísmo*, or José Vasconcelos's cosmic race, the Latin denoted a spiritual refinement rooted in millennial Greco-Roman civilization that secured Latin America's place as a utopian stage for the future of humanity. Under midcentury anti-imperialism—

liberation theology, *foquismo*, *testimonio*—it is associated as much with giving voice to local, marginalized communities as with the impending suspension of Western history through tricontinental revolution. And in its powerful revival since the advent of postcolonial studies, "Latin" acts as an appropriative watchword for all that is in and from "here"—subaltern ways of knowing, border epistemologies, the Iberian legacy of imperial modernity—and which for that reason claims at once to be radically heterogeneous to hegemonic power structures and poised to destabilize them from within. At every turn, the Latin referent oversees the double movement of mondialatinization: It attaches and detaches the identitarian ties of place and community, preserving their most sacred covenant by opening them up to machinic abstraction and global exchange. As Brett Levinson has phrased it, "The Latin American difference, even when presented as a specific alterity or identity, discloses the intrinsic heterogeneity of being, freed from the despotism of the One: a global heterogeneity that names the future liberation of mankind" ("Globalizing Paradigms," 73).

To begin with, then, mondialatinization aptly describes the fundamental discursive features of dominant Latin American(ist) production. But what makes it all the more strikingly pertinent to this dynamic, and what will mainly interest me here, is the way the theorization of this concept is emphatically linked to a "Latin" history of religion and philosophy. In "Faith and Knowledge"—a work dedicated to deciphering and dissecting the "return of religion" through contemporary forces of globalization—Derrida insists time and again on naming, dating, and remarking the particularly Latin character of his problematic, reminding us that the 1994 conference from which the book originates took place on the "Latin" island of Capri among European "Latins" speaking French, Italian, and Spanish; and announcing at the outset that before embarking on any history of religion and reason, faith and knowledge, "we must formally take note of the fact that *we are already speaking Latin*" (Derrida, "Faith and Knowledge," 74). The question of *religio*, he suggests, quite simply merges with the question of Latin. The underlying Latinity of the history of religion "remains contingent and significant at the same time. It demands to be taken into account, reflected, thematized, dated" (53). Indisputably, to Derrida's mind a formal acknowledgment and even commemoration of the Latin is in order if we are to understand the religious compulsion behind globalization.

My purpose here is to conduct a reading of "Faith and Knowledge," though I aim to draw attention not so much to the historico-thematic analogies (the centrality of Christianity, Roman heritage, and so on) that can be made to Latin Americanism, as to the ways *religio* has already structured

the possibility of speaking for any given singularity as a kind of enshrinement of the sacred. There already exist a number of compelling deconstructive critiques of Latin Americanism's own historic enshrinement of
experience, testimony, and place that unequivocally illustrate the way its
objects of study are from the beginning predicated on and sedimented in
the flows of global exchange.[2] I do not plan to dispute these but rather to
consider how their by now familiar points can be accented with a more ear-
nest consideration of the singular than even logically irrefutable conclusions about Latin America's "impossibility" or its existence qua phenomenon of globalization have so far managed to produce. Put briefly: If the
very process of deconstructing mondialatinization, on Derrida's account,
demands that we take the Latin into account, that we save its name, so to
speak, even as we pull apart the notion of salvation, how do we translate
his exhortation to the mondialatinization of Latin America?[3] My explora-
tions of this question will focus on the impossible relation Derrida locates
at the core of *religio* between faith as testimony or credit and the holy as
indemnification. A proper reckoning of this relation, I argue, requires us to
affirm deconstruction not only as a logical calculus of what remains in each
case to be deconstructed, but also and simultaneously as an experience of
the undeconstructible.

What is first observed in Derrida's mondialatinization, to the contrary
of Latinist rhetoric in Hispanism, is that it does not speak Spanish but
is expressed in an Anglo-American idiom, "like an English word that has
been to Rome and then taken a detour to the United States" (74). It refers
to the global expansion of teletechnoscience driven by the two primordial
sources of religion: on one hand, the experience of belief, credit, and trust-
worthiness; on the other, the experience of the sacrosanct, the holy, and the
unscathable. Derrida's whole point in "Faith and Knowledge" is to show
that the development of reason and science, teletechnoscience, "far from
opposing religion, bears, supports, and supposes it" (73). Mondialatinization entails religion, not only because a basic act of faith underwrites the
capitalist logic of globalization but also because telemediatic rationality, in
its expropriation of national or ethnopolitical structures, drives the resur-
gence of radical indemnification evidenced, for example, in religious and
communitarian fundamentalisms. This is why it is out of breath, *essoufflée*,
despite its apparently total colonization of the forms of exchange, knowledge, and belief today. Insofar as the sources of religion provide mondialatinization's condition and internal limit, it is propagated by the social nexus
of faith in its secular form—this is the performative "believe me" of any
address, the fiduciary link forged through language that engenders God as

its absent center, a "transcendental addressing machine" in which faith sets
the social bond in motion and continually renews it with "the production
and reproduction of the unproducible absent in place, . . . the presence of
that absence" (73).

The constitutive function of faith in mondialatinization also binds it to
a specifically Latin heritage of revelation and belief, the history that Derrida says we must account for, reflect, and thematize, by virtue of the indi-
visibility of the two sources of religion just outlined: If language through
iterability and repetition, the absent presence of God, makes belief possible in general as social nexus, it is also, as Derrida says, inseparable from
the "political, familial, ethnic, communitarian nexus, from the nation and
from the people: from autochthony, blood and soil" (52). The import of
mondialatinization's Latin provenance, the reason, in Derrida's mind, that
we should consider religion as especially Latin, thus is indebted from the
start to a double bind: on one hand, the founding prophecies and formula-
tions of the sacred in Judeo-Christian tradition inform and survive in the
general structure of the return of religion in processes of globalization;
on the other, these events as expressions of the ethnic covenant are also
indebted to the mechanical principle of faith. The Testamentary events
of Occidental monotheism—Abraham's sacrifice of Isaac, the crucifixion,
and so on—in this sense "only happen by taking on the meaning of engaging the historicity of history—and the eventfulness of the event as such"
(56). To envision this opening of history, Derrida suggests the figure of a
desert within a desert: a desertification beyond the historic sites of Middle
Eastern deserts, conjured in a performative belief that does not belong to
the set that it founds, a no-place that gives revelation its "taking place"
or "having place" (*avoir lieu*). This is what Derrida wants to signal as the
historicity of history, the eventfulness of the event engaged by the Latin
religio. The desert in the desert, a figure tied both to the messianic—an
opening of the future without horizon of expectation—and the *chora*—
that in our memory which even our memory cannot reappropriate—gives
and takes away the taking place of Latinity's history.

There is thus a dual mechanical principle at work in the mondialatinization of faith, one which "repeats again and again the double movement
of abstraction and attraction that *at the same time detaches and reattaches* to
the country, the idiom, the literal or to everything confusedly collected
today under the terms 'identity' or 'identitarian'" (86). Technoscience dis-
solves and revives the social bonds of religion: Religion does not merely
"return"—in fact, it has always been there at the heart of the logic of capitalist globalization—but turns on itself in autoimmune assault, like the

"redoubling of a wave that appropriates even that to which, enfolding it, it seems to be opposed" (89). Reading these words today, it is almost impossible not to be reminded of how Christian tenets regarding the sacredness of life are used to underwrite worldwide complexes of humanitarian aid and human rights policing in the name of a universalized, Euro-American Pax Romana, and whose same technoscientific networks feed spectacular, mediatic missions—like those of ISIS or Boko Haram—to destroy life in the name of religious restoration, a new Caliphate. The archaic forces of religion act as the gatekeepers of our cybernetic, twenty-first-century reality, producing, protecting, and annihilating its most precious charge— life, community, identity—from an irreducible distance: The new global wars of religion, as Derrida puts it, are quite literally launched *"with finger and eye."* Every subject of globalization, regardless of how privileged or remote, is also a subject of *religio*, impelled to respond to it and expose oneself to it as a primordial condition of life.

It should by now be obvious that the double movement of religion as faith and the holy or indemnified captured by the notion of mondialatinization also reprises some of Derrida's long-standing concerns with the nature of naming, testimony, signature, and event. Much of "Faith and Knowledge," as I have already noted, is engaged in asking how we can "save the name" of the sacred or historical, of the singular happenings of religion, or at least better formulate their relation to différance as a general structure of experience. Derrida articulates this problem most directly while responding to a question posed at the Villanova roundtable:

> The problem remains—and this really is a problem for me, an enigma—whether the religions, say, for instance, the religions of the Book, are but specific examples of this general structure of messianicity. There is the general structure of messianicity, as the structure of experience, and on this groundless ground there have been revelations, a history which one calls Judaism or Christianity and so on. That is a possibility and then you would have a Heideggerian gesture, in style. You would have to go back from these religions to descry the structure of messianicity on the groundless ground on which religions have been made possible. The other hypothesis—and I confess that I hesitate between these two possibilities—is that the events of revelation, the Jewish, Christian, and Islamic traditions, have been absolute events, irreducible events which have unveiled this messianicity. We would not know what messianicity is without messianism, without those events which were Abraham, Moses, and Jesus Christ, and so on. In that case singular events would have unveiled or revealed these universal

possibilities, and it is only on that condition that we can describe mes-sianicity. Between these two possibilities I must confess I oscillate and I think some other scheme has to be constructed to understand the two at the same time, to do justice to the two possibilities. (Caputo, *Decon-struction in a Nutshell*, 23–24)

Simultaneously to do justice to these two discrete and heterogeneous pos-sibilities—the originarity of the "revealed" and of "revealability"—is just what Derrida's rethinking of religion attempts to do. We can pinpoint the logic behind this effort in the way he engages the two works referenced in the subtitle of "Faith and Knowledge": Kant's *Religion within the Limits of Reason Alone* (1794) and Bergson's *The Two Sources of Morality and Religion* (1932). Derrida proposes to "condense" them to develop "the logic of what they might have let speak" (84) about religion beyond what they actually say. The two titles are significant both because they each deal with their own historical crises of the return of religion, and because they represent opposite stances on the central enigma of faith: Kant was concerned, of course, with proving its foundation in reason and Bergson with outlining its mystical sources.[4]

Kant argues that a true faith—not simply complying with the moral law but doing it always for the right reasons, with pure maxims—must be located ultimately in the autonomy of human reason. To be moral, we must behave as though God were dead, acting on a belief assured first in our freedom of thought. The principle of his religion is the same fiduciary faith or credit at work in mondialatinization, which Derrida describes at one point as "a strange alliance of Christianity, as the experience of the death of God, and techno-scientific capitalism" (65). Although this au-tonomous morality must do without the proof of revelation or miracles, becoming true through the finite, sensuous evidence of human embrace of moral laws, it nevertheless counts, in anticipation of its self-wrought salvation, on the aid of divine good will. In other words, Kant puts forth a "reflective faith" that cannot claim to know it is good but can affirm in advance, from the confines of finite experience, that it will have been "an-tecedently worthy" of God's favor.

Bergson's theory of morality in the *Two Sources* will reverse Kant's order of rational faith: For Bergson, the scrupulous fulfillment and interpretation of moral law does not secure but debase its ideals. Bergson's problem with transcendental reason is that it fails to grasp the singularity of time—it conceives as an analyzable event the progress toward salvation that in re-ality names only a retrospective illusion of the effects of change on what already exists. One cannot make one's way temporally toward the ideal, because the ideal obtains only in action, in the singular event of revelation. The sacred, in this sense, resides in the flash of mysticism, which the machine-like reproduction of reason can as easily turn toward the basest interests of social control as toward the best. The *Two Sources*, published during the interwar frenzy of industrial automatization and the escalation of interstate and imperial conflict, observes this distortion directly in the way capitalist expansion claimed to increase equality and freedom by usurping its spiritual principles. Thus does the future of religion depend for Bergson on the restitution of mysticism to rational morality—"a machine for making gods" (275).

Derrida offers only scant exegesis of Kant in "Faith and Knowledge"— and he dedicates just a few sentences to Bergson—but his bid to "condense" the two works in his title suggests that his meditations therein as a whole aim to carry the logic of each beyond their own conclusions, asking exactly what "another 'reflecting faith'" (67) or a machine that is mystical (85) would look like. This operation stems from that which both treatises have in common, namely that in their disparate attempts to reconcile the two sources of morality by eclipsing one or the other, they nonetheless maintain the absolute heterogeneity of each. The *Two Sources* is categorical on this score: It holds that religion historically oscillates between what Bergson calls "static" religion (the primitive, instinctive defense of community in ritual) and "dynamic" religion (the spiritual opening toward the totality of life). But the static cannot move toward the dynamic since the difference between them is of quality not quantity. Because time consists of change, from one to the other there is only a leap whose outcome is already in effect and whose trajectory is already gauged in the terms of "the name we give to the supposedly ultimate effect of [its] action, felt to be continuous, the hypothetical terminal point of the movement which is already sweeping us forward" (233). In the General Remarks added to the body of his *Religion* as a kind of postscript, Kant admits a similar point: The achievement of moral goodness, which "must be regarded [by reason] as nothing but an ever-during struggle toward the better," in fact "cannot be brought about through gradual reformation so long as the basis of the maxims remains impure, but must be effected through a revolution in the man's disposition. . . . He can become a new man only by a kind of rebirth, as it were a new creation . . . and a change of heart" (6:47).

The point in each case is that the difference between good and evil, between bad and good religion, cannot be "known": It occupies the future anterior; it only will have been once the revolution has crossed the absolute distance between the two. What both philosophers thus intuit but finally fail to formulate is the impossible "taking place" of religion: Transcendental idealism attempts to bridge the aporia by supplementing reason surreptitiously with divine favor; vitalism presumes the self-presence of moral energy, the élan vital. A deconstructive reading of the same problematic, of course, demonstrates the constitutive contamination of the two realms. It will show, for example, that the mystical force of revelation is the groundless condition of machinic faith, that the sacrosanct foundation of faith, in turn, is always already corrupted by the pronouncement of its promise, and that the finite labor to approximate divine goodness depends on the possibility of radical evil. That much is readily apparent. Nonetheless, the final purpose of deconstruction is not to formalize this contamination but to hold open, simultaneously and distinctly, its absolute co-constitutive possibilities. It seeks, as Derrida's earlier quote stated, to "do justice to the two possibilities" at once. This is the impossible task he refers to through Kant and Bergson in "Faith and Knowledge" ("Respect for this singular indecision or for this hyperbolic outbidding between two originarities, the order of the 'revealed' and the order of the 'revealable,' is this not at once the chance of every responsible decision and of another 'reflecting faith,' of a new 'tolerance'?" [67]), which is also assumed in the elaboration of every other concept related to ethics, justice, and responsibility. Indeed, almost every one of Derrida's later works pronounces a different iteration of this enigma: The decision, he writes in *Rogues*, "cannot be founded on or justified by any *knowledge as such*, that is, without a leap between two discontinuous and radically heterogeneous orders" (145); the act of naming, similarly, is caught between *le salut* as redemption and as call, in the "absolute heterogeneity, irreconcilable difference between the two *saluts*" ("How to Name," 130). Or again, in his remarks on the undecidability of the *chora*: "These two experiences of place, these two ways are no doubt of an absolute heterogeneity. One place excludes the other, one (sur)passes the other, one does without the other, one is absolutely, without the other" (*On the Name*, 76).

What such statements compel us to remember is not only the originary splitting of these concepts but also that deconstruction's responsibility, its chance and threat, lies in its own constitutive splitting between two possibilities. Only from within this disjunction can it do justice to the difference it hopes to hold open. Put another way: To properly affirm the two heterogeneous realms whose distinction cannot be known, deconstruction must also affirm that it *does not know*. It must comprise, as Roland Végsö puts it, a "double affirmation." The affirmation of the necessity of deconstruction always also affirms what necessarily remains undeconstructible. According to Végső, the fact that deconstruction, unlike other discourses, claims to coincide with the very condition it critiques—namely, the spacing of time that prevents the self-presence of all discourse—also means it cannot count itself exempt from that condition. There is no infinite deconstruction but only a deconstruction also suspended and interrupted by its undeconstructible limit, for although deconstruction may be exceptional, it cannot claim to be sovereign. It must also hold back in order to continue on, in what Végső calls the Sabbath of deconstruction.

We can better understand this conclusion by beginning with his logical proposition. In the terms of logic, if we consider the central assertions of deconstruction—life is difference, deconstruction is justice, experience is aporia—we begin with a judgment like no other. The statements are affirmative, but at the same time they introduce an exclusion into the identity they establish, because in stating, for example, that experience is aporia, we already accept its existence as a nonpassage, an impassibility—for there is no knowing what, if anything, comes to pass with aporia—and anticipate a following affirmation that experience is not experience at all but its opposite. The formulation is an infinite judgment—the subject is split between the infinities opened between the two affirmations submitted in the copula. What Végső wishes to acknowledge, however, is that this double infinity opened by the statement comes before its logical elaboration: "Before the propositional form of the judgment becomes possible (through the copula), the content of the judgment must be already in force: the content of the judgment precedes its form. . . . The deconstructible form of the judgment (the 'is') points toward an undeconstructible content as the condition of this deconstruction" ("Affirmative Judgments," 79). For the affirmation that experience is aporia, experience must be thought as nonpassage before we can think of it of as passage or undergoing. Similarly, if life is différance, life must first be thought as trace before being can be determined as presence. The priority of the content that conditions deconstructive formulation, the absence of presence that différance, deconstruction, and aporia affirm, cannot itself be deconstructed—it is rather deconstruction's limit. At the moment when the projection of presence is interrupted—when law no longer applies and faith no longer makes belief, deconstruction has also ceased. It must then advance two antithetical propositions: First, "nothing is inherently deconstructible," but also "there is something of the undeconstructible" (80).

It is not coincidental that Végső regards this double affirmation as an experience of the undeconstructible: It is logical to conclude, following

his foregoing arguments, that in honoring the irreducibility of aporia—
precisely the aporia as the general structure of experience—deconstruction coincides with the conditions of experience, and forcibly experiences
them.[5] Remembering that religion is defined in "Faith and Knowledge"
as "the experience of belief, on the one hand" (77), and "the experience
of the unscathed, of sacredness or of holiness, on the other" (78), it stands
to determine how exactly deconstruction is supposed to experience it. Its
endeavor to hold open these two experiences, which as we have seen are
constitutively entwined, must operate in the ellipsis between them, where
the defense of the sacred opens out in autoimmune gesture toward belief.
What is protected above all in sacredness is the dignity of human life, as
exemplified by the primacy of sacrifice in the history of revelation—it is
in appropriating its other, nonlife, that sacrifice preserves the value of life,
since, in Derrida's words, "life has absolute value only if it is *more than
life*. . . . It is sacred, holy, infinitely respectable only in the name of what
is more than it" (94), so that the price of human life is truly priceless. The
holy must preserve and reproduce this more than itself, the death it appropriates, in a performative repetition that "reproduces with the regularity
of a technique the instance of the non-living or, if you prefer, of the dead
in the living" (94). The automatic safeguarding of the life of the sacred also
performs its incessant interruption: not just a sacrifice, says Derrida, but a
self-sacrifice, a *halte*, holding back or reticence, which responds not only
to reverence for the holy but also to the autoimmunity that keeps it alive,
thus "open to something other and more than itself: the other, the future,
death, freedom, the coming or the love of the other, the space and time of
a spectralizing messianicity beyond all messianism" (95). Would the deconstruction of religion, conceived on the order of experience, not also
be precisely such a self-sacrifice, holding itself back in respect before the
possibility of the sacred, on the one hand, and the opening to messianicity,
on the other, exactly that which is undeconstructible in religion?[6] In this
suspension deconstruction would also then inexorably partake of religion
and faith, which is what Végső no doubt intimates when he refers to it as
a Sabbath.

  What I have tried to highlight in the motif of self-sacrifice or holding
back is the way that, in confronting its own conditions of possibility—
différance as absolute heterogeneity—deconstruction summons restraint
as before the sacred, before that which must remain intact or unscathed. It
therefore cannot be, as Martin Hägglund has it, a radical atheism. Hägglund limits the infinite deferral of différance to what he calls the "infinite
finitude of life": for him "messianic hope . . . is a hope for temporal sur-

vival, faith is always faith in the finite, and the desire for God is a desire for the mortal" (*Radical Atheism*, 120). On this view, the originary spacing of time that prevents self-presence overdetermines im-possibility from the start—immunity *as such* is not merely im-possible but unthinkable. This premise leads to Hägglund's reading of salvation, which he must qualify as follows:

> Insofar as salvation is understood as the absolute immunity of immortality, it is out of the question. There can be no such salvation, since nothing can happen without the greeting of an other that can come to compromise any immunity. However, insofar as salvation is understood as a survival that saves one from death by giving one more time to live, it is not out of the question. (131)[7]

We confront here two salvations, one unimaginable, undesirable, out of the question, and another that is merely im-possible. Yet if we are to take seriously Derrida's pretension to do justice, separately, to both poles of the radical heterogeneity it addresses, then deconstruction cannot make such a qualification. The modal difference between immortality and finitude is itself integral to this heterogeneity, proven by the fact that each time we renew faith through survival, redemption has not come. By subsuming this not-coming to its theorization, by affirming solely a spacing of time that limits salvation to survival, deconstruction makes just one affirmation: It affirms deconstruction as its own horizon, its own infinity. But unlike différance, deconstruction is as finite as what it deconstructs and must therefore hope to live on, by coming to and affirming its own end.

Let us go back now to the remarks I first made about Latin Americanism's fervent belief in the singularity of its referent. Hägglund's reading of salvation is an apposite point at which to return to that question because it closely echoes the conclusions of a certain deconstructive critique of Latin Americanism that has become familiar and influential in recent years: to wit, that the representation of any experience, no matter how silenced or Other, is subject to the effects of deferral and universalization that make representation possible, and that furthermore, to imagine a subject of any kind—indigenous, revolutionary, popular, and so on—that could resist these conditions of possibility from some perspective radically exterior to it is to imagine nothing at all, because such a perspective could not exist. Or worse, Hägglund tells us, it would be to imagine radical evil, a total stasis where neither resistance nor salvation could ever come to pass. We must therefore accept, a priori, that Latin Americanism, or that which it names, is impossible. David E. Johnson, to cite just one example, arrives at such a conclusion: "Insofar as Latin America is named, it is in name only, which means Latin America is not in itself; it is not proper to itself or as such. Latin America belongs therefore neither to itself nor to any other. Rather, Latin American Studies is impossible, but no less necessary for this impossibility, because it is unlocatable. Indeed, its discovery or invention, that is, its having been named, by anyone and everyone, depends on its impossible location" ("How (Not) to Do Latin American Studies," 16).

In the argument itself, of course, there is nothing to impugn. Its verdict is perfectly logical and true to the fundamental precepts of deconstruction. My doubt, and hope, does not concern the correctness of this sort of reading but how to shift its constative impetus toward the experiential register it hides, to account for Latin America's impossible unlocatability not as the always already split possibility of a proper name, but doubly at once as a chance between its singular occurrence and its total dispersion. As I have argued, this would amount for Derrida to doing justice to what in the name Latin America remains undeconstructible.

How could the calculating operation of deconstruction be infused with the added affirmation of its experience, of its holding open before that which will not be divulged? It would be something like reading a shibboleth, a watchword for a secret belonging. In an essay titled "Shibboleth," Derrida explores at length the various connotations of this figure: It serves as a password to distinguish ally from enemy in times of war, a cut or partition that, as in circumcision, names the event of legitimate entry into a community; in addition, as a cut, the shibboleth also cuts off the singularity of any name or date from its silence or ruin. The power of partition—Derrida means to exploit the dual meaning of *partager* as "to divide" and "to share"—signals the shibboleth's existence first and foremost as a happening. Because its meaning is arbitrary, empty—like the memorable "Hispanic" shibboleth *perejil* that decided the 1937 massacre of Haitians in Hispaniola—its truth is made in an absolute decision: Either one can pronounce it or they cannot, and the outcome of its trial irrevocably creates the alternative of inclusion or exclusion, life or death. For the same reason, Derrida remarks, the shibboleth cannot be properly known but only made. Its constative and performative functions are held resolutely separate, related without relation. So it is as well with language: "What enters and incises language in the form of a date, is that there is a partaking of the shibboleth, a partaking at once open and closed. The date (signature, moment, place, gathering of singular marks) always operates as a shibboleth. It shows that there is something not shown, that there is ciphered singularity: irreducible to any concept, to any knowledge, even to a history or tradition, be it of a religious kind" ("Shibboleth," 33). What "there is" in his description, it must be noted, is not the singularity itself of any signature, but the absolute heterogeneity of the shibboleth's "terrifying ambiguity . . . indiscernible discernment between alliance and war" (48). We partake of what is ciphered there twice, once in entrance to its covenant and once sundered from it before its inscrutability, living each chance separately and simultaneously. The shibboleth thus has a secret readability, like the *no pasarán* of the Spanish Republic, a "handclasp, a rallying cipher, a sign of membership" (23) that is legible only to the chosen—and as with salvation, we do not know we are saved until it has always already happened. Deconstruction can refuse to sacralize the object of Latin American studies while continuing to affirm the ambiguity of its secret, partaking without knowledge of what is still there in the Latin. From there it will remain open to the coming of the life that is left in the machine of mondialatinization.

NOTES

1. Derrida's neologism *mondialatinization* underscores the sense of a "world," not necessarily physical, communicated by the French *monde*—which, as Jean-Luc Nancy avers, is replaced in the English "globe" by the sense of "an enclosure in the undifferentiated sphere of a unitotality" (*Creation of the World*, 28). In his English translation of Derrida's "Faith and Knowledge," Samuel Weber proposes "globalatinization," noting that, while the emphasis on earthly space conveyed by the English obscures Derrida's distinction between earth and world, the fact of Anglo-American dominance witnessed by the very translation of *mondialatinization* forces us to consider the larger epistemological issue of "what happens to the notion of 'world' . . . if the predominant language of 'mondialatinization' tends to speak not of 'world' but of 'globality'" (109). Because my focus here is on the singular dimension of the Latin highlighted by Derrida, I have chosen to maintain his original French term. On the question of translation of notions of world and globalization, see also chapter 5 of Emily Apter's *Against World Literature*.

2. To name just a few: Scott Michaelsen and Scott Cutler Shershow, "Rethinking Border Thinking" (which appeared together with Brett Levinson's and David E. Johnson's essays that I quote above and below in the special issue of *South Atlantic Quarterly* "Latin America in Theory," and which also can be counted as the type of deconstructive reading I am referring to); Alberto Moreiras's *The Exhaustion of Difference*; Gareth Williams's *The Other Side of the Popular*; and Abraham Acosta's *Thresholds of Illiteracy*.

3. My use of this phrase is meant to retain the primary association it has in Derrida's discussion of negative theology—that of the sacrifice involved in keeping the name safe by saving all except (save) the name.

4. Kant published *Reason* shortly after the ascension of Frederick William II and the subsequent curtailment of religious freedom, including the requirement of formal confession of faith for all theology candidates and public censorship (see Shell, *Kant and the Limits of Autonomy*, 186–88); Bergson's *Two Sources* appeared concomitantly with the rise of Nazism and on the crest of post-WWI commercial expansion. The contexts of their publication are thus directly reflected in Kant's repudiation of "dogmatic" faith and Bergson's trepidation before the "frenzy" of industrial growth, which he saw as a sign of a bloated but static state of religion.

5. See Végső, "Deconstruction and Experience," for a thorough demonstration of the experiential dimension of deconstruction.

6. Rei Terada ("Scruples," 256) infers a similar suggestion in Derrida's motif of self-sacrifice.

7. What Derrida says here, in "How to Name," is "It is necessary that *le salut* of salvation or health, *le salut* of redemption or resurrection never be assured. Not that it is out of the question, but it is necessary that it always could be refused, threatened, forbidden, lost, gone" (130).

WORKS CITED

Acosta, Abraham. *Thresholds of Illiteracy: Theory, Latin America, and the Crisis of Resistance*. New York: Fordham University Press, 2014.

Apter, Emily. *Against World Literature: On the Politics of Untranslatability*. New York: Verso, 2013.

Bergson, Henri. *The Two Sources of Morality and Religion*. Translated by R. Ashley Audra and Cloudesley Brereton. London: Macmillan, 1935.

Caputo, John. *Deconstruction in a Nutshell: A Conversation with Jacques Derrida*. New York: Fordham University Press, 1997.

Derrida, Jacques. "Faith and Knowledge." Translated by Samuel Weber. In *Acts of Religion*, edited by Gil Anidjar, 1–39. New York: Routledge, 2002.

———. "How to Name." In *Recumbents*, by Michel Deguy, translated by Wilson Baldridge, 191–221. Middletown, Conn.: Wesleyan University Press, 2005.

———. *On the Name*. Edited by Thomas Dutoit. Translated by David Wood, John P. Leavey Jr., and Ian McLeod. Stanford: Stanford University Press, 1993.

———. *Rogues: Two Essays on Reason*. Translated by Pascale-Anne Brault and Michael Naas. Stanford: Stanford University Press, 2005.

————. "Shibboleth." In *Sovereignties in Question: The Poetics of Paul Celan*, edited by Thomas Dutoit and Outi Pasanen, 1–64. New York: Fordham University Press, 2005.

Hägglund, Martin. *Radical Atheism: Derrida and the Time of Life*. Stanford: Stanford University Press, 2008.

Johnson, David E. "How (Not) to Do Latin American Studies." *South Atlantic Quarterly* 106, no. 1 (2007): 1–16.

Kant, Immanuel. *Religion within the Limits of Reason Alone*. Translated by Theodore M. Greene and Hoyt H. Hudson. New York: Harper Torchbooks, 1960.

Levinson, Brett. "Globalizing Paradigms, or The Delayed State of Latin American Theory." *South Atlantic Quarterly* 106, no. 1 (2007): 61–83.

Michaelsen, Scott, and Scott Cutler Shershow. "Rethinking Border Thinking." *South Atlantic Quarterly* 106, no. 1 (2007): 39–60.

Moreiras, Alberto. *The Exhaustion of Difference. The Politics of Latin American Cultural Studies*. Durham, NC: Duke University Press, 2001.

Nancy, Jean-Luc. *The Creation of the World, or Globalization*. Translated by François Raffoul and David Pettigrew. Albany: State University of New York Press, 2007.

Shell, Susan Meld. *Kant and the Limits of Autonomy*. Cambridge, Mass.: Harvard University Press, 2009.

Terada, Rei. "Scruples, or Faith in Derrida." *South Atlantic Quarterly* 106, no. 2 (2007): 237–64.

Végső, Roland. "Affirmative Judgments: The Sabbath of Deconstruction." *parallax* 16, no. 3 (2010): 74–84.

————. "Deconstruction and Experience: The Politics of the Undeconstructible." In *A Leftist Ontology: Beyond Relativism and Identity Politics*, edited by Carsten Strathausen, 125–46. Minneapolis: University of Minnesota Press, 2009.

Williams, Gareth. *The Other Side of the Popular: Neoliberalism and Subalternity in Latin America*, Durham, N.C.: Duke University Press, 2002.

PART II

Form and Secrecy

CHAPTER 4

The Jew or Patriarchy (or Worse)

Brett Levinson

In the essay "Abraham, the Other," largely centered on a reading of Sartre's 1946 *Anti-Semite and Jew*, Derrida notes that, since the Jew as such does not exist, the figure of the marrano is no less a Jew than the Jew, and may even be more so: "That is why I play seriously, more and more, with the figure of the marrano: the less you show yourself as jewish, the more and better jew you will be" (13). The Jew, argues Sartre via Derrida's reconstruction, is not so because he or she belongs to this or that history, possesses this or that biological feature, or is this or that type of Jew. The Jew is a Jew due to no property but because he or she inherits at birth, without meriting it, an external debt, the call or law of the Other, as the condition of existence. Thus, a marrano with no Jewish record, not even a hidden, forgotten or denied one—one, for instance, who enters the Jewish situation merely because accused by the neighbor for economic reasons: in fifteenth- and sixteenth-century Spain, such accusations were common[1]—makes the strongest claim on Judaism. This name-calling from the outside, such as the one to which Borges responds in the essay "I, a Jew," is Jewishness itself. The distinction between what I call myself, "I, a Jew," and what the Other calls me—one thinks of Woody Allen's anxiety when interpellated by "Jew eat?" in the film "Annie Hall"—between subjectivity and subjection, is unjewish. In fact, when I call myself a Jew due to my Jewish properties, I am distant from my Judaism since, in such a case, I take the endowment of language that the call of the Other incarnates as my ownmost, hence annul its (the call's) Otherness—annul the Judaism that is in me more than myself.

Though without a definitive characteristic, the Jew can emerge, according to Derrida's analysis of Sartre, as authentic or inauthentic. There exist Jews who affirm without shame the nonproperty of their existence, hence are authentic; and inauthentic Jews who accept the call, "hey, jew!," their assimilation into the nation-state, as that authenticity. The latter mistake their alienation, their immersion into an abstract universality such as capitalism or nationalism for the truth of their situation. This Jew, states Sartre in different terms, sees himself or herself as a man. And "man," the abstract universal, does not for Sartre exist since "man" is without historical situation. Notwithstanding, "man" serves as the inauthentic Jew's means of measure or devaluation. He or she "eradicates" his or her Jewishness by assuming the identity of a "man" "for the benefit of *man*. But *man* does not exist. There are Jews, Protestants, Catholics; there are Frenchmen, Englishmen, Germans; there are whites, blacks, yellows" (Sartre, *Anti-Semite and Jew*, 144–45).

Sartre's "man [who] does not exist," then, is the condition of the elements that do exist, just as valueless money, in Marx, is the condition of all values. Blacks, Jews, and others, contrasted with the "man who is not," are actualities: specific men in specific situations. Within Saussurean linguistics, one signifier is distinct from another only within a closed, abstract system (such as "English," whose "actual territory" could never be defined but is an abstraction). Similarly, Blacks and Jews are specific "ethnicities" by virtue of the abstraction "man," which closes the set: binds, divides, determines, and, at the same time, *disavows* these peoples. Thus, black, in Sartre's assertion, is obviously not a color. Color is a modifier, never an actuality. Black is someone who, negating his or her abstraction, finds himself or herself in a specific historical situation: that of black people. Similarly the Jew, not enjoying the property of a religion, race, nation, is Jewish only insofar as he or she is *not* a "man." Thus, had Sartre's list included, among "Jews, blacks, and yellows," *blues and magentas*, that is, had the philosopher failed to petition the abstraction *man*, the list (imagine the inventory "magenta, Jew, yellow," which would not be a register of men) would be an idiotic muddle rather than a set of different or even alienated groups. It would be senseless—it would be, that is, if "man" were not replaced by an alternative abstraction. And, according to Derrida, such a substitution always takes place (and not only in Sartre), which substitute has a name: the signifier. Even absent a reference to *man*, yellow, Jew, magenta, beans, form a meaningful whole through their abstract common: They are all signifiers. Stated differently, the universal on which Sartre speculates is the *signifier* "man"—the signifier and "man," which consequently serve as the condition of possibility of both the meaning of, and partition between his categories, in the case at hand, between the authentic and inauthentic Jew.

Sartre's theory of the Jew and anti-Semitism thus generates a quagmire. A black person is not so due to skin color—appearing white, he or she can be perfectly black—but because called and calling himself or herself black, that is, owing a debt to what Lacan calls the Symbolic Order (or the Other), the order, not of language, but of signifiers. Thus, if the Jew too *is* because he or she inherits a debt that arrives with the call of the Other, blacks are no less Jews than Jews: We are all Jews.

Hence, the Jew in Sartre's analysis would serve as the example of human subjectivity as such: "Here, exemplarism would consist in acknowledging, or claiming to identify, in what one calls the Jew the exemplary figure of a universal structure of the living human, to wit, this being originally indebted, responsible, guilty" (Derrida, "Abraham," 12). This thesis concerning the Jew as example of general "man," the "man" without qualities or specificity, is the main object of Derrida's critique in "Abraham, the Other." He indicates that every nationalism appeals to such a notion of the example, "nationalism never having been the claim to particularity or to an irreducible difference but rather a vocation for universal exemplarity, and therefore a responsibility without limits, for every one and in front of every one" (ibid.). Even Celan, says Derrida, submits to the temptation of a "Jewish exemplarity" (ibid.). Derrida does not, in this discussion, mention Slavoj Žižek, but he might have. Indeed, for Žižek, the Jew represents an example, a model figure of abjection, the subject that is crossed out by the Symbolic order, which figure any type or individual can occupy. Hence, in one of Žižek's interviews, titled "It Doesn't Have to Be a Jew," Žižek presents the Jew as the prototype of a certain foreign, threatening subject, inheritor and carrier of a certain foreign "thing," which "carrier" is the universal subject, that is, the being with no property but that of signifier, which every subject inherits. The Jew embodies the uncanniness of the subject that every subject is.

In fact, Derrida warns, if the propertyless Jew exemplifies "universal man," he or she is not a particular, hence not a Jew. Is the situation, then, that the Jew embodies, for Derrida, an aporia, perhaps aporia itself? Yet one could name *aporia* every figure. "Woman," for example. Like the Jew, "woman" possesses no language, nation, consciousness, history, and certainly no biological feature that she can call, by nature, her own. She is "woman" by means of an accusation or call by the Other, which negates her. Thus Lacan's "woman does not exist" (*Encore*, 7): woman can only name herself from the site of the big Other. "Anti-essentialist" woman, then, is like the Jew, without qualities. A woman for being exemplified by the essential-less Jew, woman is a Jew for being a man. And should woman, as a particular, fail to embody the universal, fail to be the "man" that disavows her existence—fail, in other words, to occupy the place of the mother, the one supposed to be All—she enjoys her womanhood even less. Either woman/Jew is inscribed into patriarchy, into the father or *père*; or her situation is worse or *pire*, in which case she claims an absolute inessentiality: expendability. In desiring an other-than-patriarchy, woman gains less-than-patriarchy. She emerges as the whore rather than the mother, receiving a full bowl of the father plus an extra serving. *Père ou pire* (the main discussion of Lacan's *Le Seminaire, Livre XIX . . . ou pire*): abstract nonexistence or worse.

Not only Jews, then, but blacks, women, queers, and so on: All such bodies exemplify equally the aporia of subjectivity. Either the I is, in which case it is not; or it is not, in which case it is not. Aporia, then, does not represent Derrida's last word on the subject of the Jew in "Abraham, the Other." Quite to the contrary, it represents Sartre's last word as conceived by Derrida, the very view that Derrida eventually dismantles. Sartre arrives at the position, according to Derrida, by conflating the signifier, the universal, and "man." Only if man is a signifier can the Jew exemplify the aporia of universality, hence of the "living human." In such a case, though, this aporia not only fails to be a universal; it fails to be an aporia. After all, if aporia is the truth of subjectivity, it is not an aporia, an obstruction that submits to no answer, but is that answer, the truth of the subject.

The Jew, phrased differently, cannot exemplify the *non-lieu* of human subjectivity since *non-lieu*, the landless exile that is for existentialism the condition of modern man, is a signifier, a *lieu*, as well as an abstract whole that gives place to all places. Indeed, if the DP, the displaced person or Jew, in 1946 (when Sartre wrote his treatise on the Jew), were the example of man in his existential homelessness, he or she would be, in bad times, held responsible for the illness, be made an example of the man he exemplifies, pay as scapegoat for the sins of a mankind that redeems itself through the annihilation of that example—if this were Derrida's argument, we would not need Derrida to make it for we have all heard elsewhere, pre-deconstruction, the story of a Jew who is made an example of man, and who, murdered, cleanses the "living human."

Thus, Derrida's main concern, in "Abraham," is not the Jew as example, or man as example, not even the example "as such" but—in order to address the "Jewish question"—the "example" of the signifier, example *as* signifier. The issue at hand, stated differently, is not the signifier *of* totality but the signifier *as* totality. When we cast the whole as the sum of signifiers plus the lack of the signifier for that whole, a lack such as "man" which, by faultily accounting for the totality (does anyone still believe that "man" accounts without fault for the whole of being?), discloses its own insufficiency (as do all signifiers: all represent the lack of a transcendental signifier, so that lack pertains to every element of the Symbolic order, thus *is* the universal)—in such a case, "lack" names, systematizes, and renders meaningful the series. In making such a gesture, we posit being in terms of representation, that is, in terms of presence: the actuality or being that representation *merely* reflects, and which, as epiphenomenal reflection, is in truth being, presence, the "living human."

Obviously, Derrida's critique is indirectly directed at a certain Lacanianism, which would imagine a "signifier without a signified." Derrida argues that, because the signifier results from iteration and convention (the "arbitrariness of the sign") no less than the signified does ("cat," to be sure, represents the signified "furry animal that meows" due to arbitrary rituals; yet "cat" is a *signifier*, as opposed to unsystematic marks or haphazard noises, due to the same rituals), the signifier (without signified) *is* the signified, just as mimesis is eidos. This point is especially crucial for any understanding of the marrano. For the marrano is not a secret Jew, a Spanish converso who clandestinely performed Jewish rituals, whose heresy was discovered or not. It is not a signifier that reveals or conceals a true signified, essence, or body. I suggested above why this is the case. In the brutal political and economic situation that was the Spanish Inquisition, Old Christians could be denounced as marranos hence endure the marrano situation as marranos. Conversely, conversos who not only did not practice Judaism, but did not even remember that their ancestors once did (or may have), could be accused of "marranismo." Depicting no true meaning, "marrano," then, might too easily be taken as a signifier without signified, a "floating" signifier. Obviously, though, such an interpretation would be incorrect, even ideological. The signifier "marrano" exists because operating within a string, system, or context—Jew, converso, New Christian, Old Christian, Christian, pig, marrano, and so on—which renders "marrano" meaningful rather than nonsensical, a signified over a signifier, even given the possible absence of a true or fixed meaning. As signifier, "marrano" is a signified and subject, still one more embodiment of the "living human" (who, as example of man, can be sacrificed for the overall good).

Derrida offers numerous names for this reduction of being (or language) to representation, hence to the meaningful: patriarchy, humanism, logocentrism, metaphysics, nationalism, and, of course, subjectivity. I have emphasized that, without a signifier for the whole, without an artificial frame, even that of "signifier," a succession of words is not even a succession, much less meaningful, but worse. Thus, absent a universal signifier, a subject, if a subject, will still appeal to the signifier. It will fend off the *pire* by turning it back into a reflection of the *père*, the father who, lacking (the signifier of lack), is all the more present, all the more powerful, the guarantee that all is reducible to (self)representation, the living human.

This does not mean that a transcendental figure, absent or present, is an illusion, like God, that is nonetheless necessary for being. Lack and the signifier (which, again, are one and the same, since every signifier signifies the lack of a transcendental signifier) is essential, not for being, but for meaning. Lack serves to disavow the threat of nonmeaning, of the being and saying that are irreducible to signification. That which is missing from meaning offers the possibility of the recovery of that loss. Lack is the guarantee of possible fulfillment or wholeness.

Such Derridean premises, staged in "Abraham, the Other," are especially important for an understanding of today's geopolitical scene. Our anomic situation, after all, is not that being, with no sign of the universal—democracy, civilization, globalization, the West, and *man* and *Jew* (as in "we are all German Jews")[2] obviously fail—is meaningless and valueless. It is worse, for global circumstances result from non-lack, from a surplus that possesses no sign: the terrorist, the drug-trafficker, the illegal migrant (as opposed to the political refugee), the homeless, pandemics. All of these are figures that, potentially, cannot be identified, possessing no sign. A truck conveying avocados, which crosses from Ciudad Juárez into San Antonio, may be one that conveys avocados or smuggles cocaine; the Muslim woman who puts down a big bag in the New York subway may be either a devout woman who simply finds her luggage too heavy or a terrorist; the Syrian desperately fleeing a horrific political predicament in search of refugee status may be an unfortunate Syrian or a wealthy Serbian whose interest is the economic benefit of living in Germany. The woman as devout Muslim (if we may focus on this particular example), through her dress, is the repetition or copy of a set of rituals. The same woman as terrorist repeats or copies those repetitions. The difference is not between actuality and representation, true and false, or signified and signifier, but between two repetitions, that is, without sign. There is a profound, an unqualified difference. Yet there is no signifier of the difference, for the signifier, the signs, generate in the first place the confusion, the indifference.

"Cat" represents "furry animal that meows" through iteration, habit, and the conventions of a linguistic tradition that are deployed by living humans. Yet "cat" never represents or means the repetition that it is. Repetition (re-presentation) withdraws from representation, signification. Likewise, the difference between the Syrian refugee with a proper ID and the wealthy Serbian with a fake ID, cannot be told, narrated, for the difference falls between repetitions, dropping from representation. And this is precisely what the marrano marks and yet does not exemplify, according to Derrida. The false copy of a false copy (the bad version of the converso, who is a bad version of the Old Christian), marrano is not a signifier, or not merely a signifier but an indication of the irreducibility of being to the signifier, which irreducibility is repetition. The embodiment of a repetition that cannot be separated from another repetition, cannot necessarily be identified, like the migrant who keeps coming and coming and coming into the European Union (as I write on September 22, 2015), the marrano, without sign, menaces as that which cannot even be erased. A signifier, as well as the subject that it always already identifies, is divided between the representation that appears (and conceals) and the iteration that withdraws, hence is never the same as itself, never signifier. Insofar as the signifier is a signifier, it is a signified or subject; yet a signifier is never just a signifier, but as well a repetition, always more than a signifier. Therefore, the signifier that, as lack, "wholes" the universe of signifiers into a signifying array, disbands the whole by adding an extra that extends endlessly the domain, disunifying it, endangering its meaningfulness, the possibility of identifying all parts. The marrano, iteration of the Jew/Christian, is the signifier of a domain that is not composed of signifiers, that resists identification, and therefore must be identified to death—targeted as the figure and promise of death to all rather than (as signifier) as the assurance of the life of the whole, of the "living humans."

Let us take a step back. Marx argues that money, stupid paper, enjoys no worth in and of itself, just as Sartre contends that man does not exist. Yet if one eradicates this abstract equivalent, this lack in reality (money), which founds all value, one removes also all other values: peace, love, understanding, freedom, judgment. That these "goods" have been converted by capitalism into calculations, into capital, into the *père*, may seem, or be, atrocious. Yet without the calculations matters appear worse, *pire*, for then one is without meaning or measure to make evaluations of any sort. Either there are bad universal values or no values, the harmful versus the good or no manner in which to ascertain the difference, signifiers and identity politics or worse. The *père*, the *nom du père*, the *nom*, the name, the signifier, lack, signification, are not essential, not even to language. They are means to fend off the more dreadful, which is the repetition, the will not cease and will not cease and will not cease, which withdraws from signification. In fact, however, the *pire*, the worse that is the limit of representation may not be bad. It may be the jouissance about which meaning and subjectivity want to know nothing.

Patriarchy, capitalism, signification, and subjectivity are not necessary. Why then do they return generation after generation as if they were? They return because desired, because chosen over that which is more dangerous. The subject prefers meaning to nonsense or joy, the *père* to the *pire*. In fact, one cannot act in the interest of the good, safe, and meaningful without putting into play the most dangerous and terrible, the extra that disbands every totality. The "living humans" of patriarchy, akin to Hegel's slave, opt for signification over the open, subjectivity over exposure, security over the death, as they are frightened of their own freedom.

Paul de Man labels this "option" ideology. Indeed, de Man's famous definition of ideology, "the confusion of linguistic with natural reality, of reference with phenomenalism" (*Resistance to Theory*, 11), refers to precisely this: the confusion of logic and meaning (natural reality and phenomenalism) for being and essence (linguistic reality, reference). The counter to meaning, hence ideology, is for de Man reading. Reading demands, says de Man, the imposition of a figure. *On the one hand*, this figure cannot fail to arise as a signifier, umbrella of an imaginary or artificial whole. Without this figure, without rhetoric as signifier and subject, one cannot apprehend—much less comprehend—an articulation or text. The trope as signifier allows being and language to be cast, arbitrarily, as a finite field of representation, hence as the reflection of natural reality or phenomenalism. The reflection or image, though nothing real, is not nothing. It is "actuality": de Man's ideology results from the mix-up of the linguistic and representation, which in turns gives way to "the confusion of linguistic with natural reality." Ideology, in other words, results not from false consciousness but from consciousness, from the signifier that yields (self)representation: from the "confusion" of consciousness and totality which the figure breeds.

This is not to suggest that thinking, or what de Man, and the Derrida of "Plato's Pharmacy" (and elsewhere) call reading, are other than meaning or ideology. I noted above that the signifier no less than the signified emerges by virtue of convention, repetition. I just suggested, as well, that a figure or trope is necessarily also a signifier. Yet a trope—and this is de Man's *on the other hand*—is also a sign that represents another sign, thus re-presents repetition. "Teeth" is an abstraction that unifies, repeats, abstracts, figures all the distinct biting instruments in my mouth. "Pearls" repeat this repetition. Therefore, a certain mechanicity, a repetition not of free will, but of a program that is itself mechanical, a repetition, pertains to "human" language. A machine repeats, and is not free not to continue repeating. A trope, likewise, repeats a system of signification, a logic that results from tradition or ritual, and that operates regardless of all human subjectivity. De Man's "figure" represents repetition rather than the subject of representation. It thereby names the difference of the subject from itself, the signifier (split between repetition and representation) from itself, human life from itself. Human life, mechanical, "unlive," is not itself, at least not all of itself.

When the subject conveys a message by means of a trope, through a sign that does not fall easily into the common sense, that message is received by another in a fashion that cannot be predicted. The "deconstructionist" argument is not that, in speaking, "anything can happen": The sign can "mean whatever" owing to the force and desire of the receiver (whether actual or imagined, present or absent). The point is that, the subject is exposed to the limit of its own force by virtue of the speech that represents it. Because repetition, mechanicity, is the condition of communication, communication does not obey the will of "human lives." Why exactly not? Because in communicating or representing itself, the subject, nonmaster of iteration or communication, runs into its limit. That limit, in turn, is a contact zone. It is site of contamination, one where the Same is touched or dirtied by the Other, speaker by whatever receiver. Given the boundary without which there is no subject, representation, or homogeneity, the Other is already always internal to Sameness—subject, signifier—which is thus not the Same as itself. "Rhetoric" does not concern good or bad, literary or literal speech/writing. Nor does it "boil down" to the thesis that the power of the speaker/author must yield to the force of the listener/reader. At stake is the fact that communication of "meaning" is never not the communication of "disease." The conveyance of meaning inserts a limit between subject and Other, which limit introduces into the signifying apparatus that which is foreign to this signifier, foreign to being and well-being. The subject can neither produce nor impede this contamination; the I is neither source nor master. Infection happens automatically (de Man would say) or unconditionally (as Derrida would say), as it cannot not happen. Every signifier, which is a sign and signified through its repetition, repeats itself as perversion that represents no subject and no object but an inhumanity that cannot be mastered by live humans. The repetition is what occurs to human representation without belonging to it since, as with a machine such as Frankenstein's monster, it goes and goes and goes, quite apart from what humans, the "makers" of the repetition, do and say.

I return, then, to terrorism, drug-trafficking, and migration, as these activities haunt contemporary geopolitics. Such pursuits take place because of an extra, nonsubjective force: the border. The boundary supplements them, which therefore do not fit into an idiom, culture, civilization, or identity, hence any process of identification, monitoring, vigilance, law, or order. The case is not that extant borders, a kind of standing reserve of power, render such movement and movements strange and menacing. Rather, the pursuits put into play these borderlands (as I write, migration throughout the European Union is generating novel divisions within Europe), hence the foreignness—the border that does not belong to any nation or nationalism—that is the condition of the homeland: speech and understanding, message and translation. The one cannot do without the other; the subject cannot emerge without the alien, for the condition of all is the crossover that pertains to no one, but exceeds each and every. The threat that does not appeal to the subject is the very one to which the subject cannot fail to appeal. Either the subject rids itself of the unfamiliar, judged to be a source of harm and danger, in which case it rids itself of itself, deconstructs itself; or it does not, in which case it opens itself to that very harm, thereby to its destruction and deconstruction once more. Either patriarchy, which accepts as legitimate only tradition, which tradition is founded on the boundaries that betray and ruin it; or the nonsubject, which removes from the range of society and politics a sign that distinguishes same and other, just and unjust, which nonsign ruins once more. These last differences—between just and unjust, harmful and good—are lost; because unsigned, because the manifestations of the repetition, the "it will not stop" that withdraws, they remain to be read or thought.

This means that no subject, neither as speaker nor listener, author nor reader, ever itself suffers or experiences the limit, the contagion, the communication of communication. The point holds because, as already signaled, the condition of human experience, even of suffering, is consciousness. And the condition of consciousness, at least according to the thinkers that I have been discussing in this essay—Derrida, de Man, and Lacan—is the signifier that renders conceivable apprehension and comprehension. The trope that turns the signifier away from the subject's mastery is also, necessarily, to repeat, the signifier and signified, the meaning, which represents that subject. The subject, in order to be, represses the force of language, of the communication between self and other, by translating the between into self-reflection, into itself (the subject, human lives). The signifier sends away language and repetition, the inhuman; consciousness forces them into withdrawal, just as the difference between Jew and marrano, Muslim and terrorist, capitalist importer and drug-trafficker, refugee and migrant, is always already off-scene and ob-scene. And that withdrawal (of repetition), without which there is no signifier, is accounted for—if there is subjectivity and signs, the unaccountable must be accounted for—by ideology. Ideology is an account of that which withdraws from all accounts. The subject, stated differently, cannot read signs but can only see or intuit them, subsume them into consciousness. The I reads the withdrawal of the sign, the withdrawal or suffering of metaphysics. Thus, theory is the resistance to the theory, de Man concludes in *The Resistance to Theory* (19), because it attends to withdrawal by narrating it, by turning repetition into representation, which representation reinstantiates the repetition that withdraws, and that re-demands reading. Every signifier is the story of the carrier that the signifier and subject cannot carry off.

I said that contagion and repetition cannot happen to a subject, since the subject or signifier is the disavowal of such an event. Contagion still happens, however. It just happens to happen to language, which happening deconstruction reads by supplementing language with more linguistic events. The representation of the alien is iterated in the writing of deconstruction. De Man's definition of ideology, "the confusion of linguistic with natural reality, of reference with phenomenalism," does not modify the idea or practice of ideology as understood by Marx. It modifies the language of ideology. As de Man casts "natural reality" as the unreal, and the linguistic as the material, he casts language as the material event that any comprehension of ideology must now strive to translate—insofar as that comprehension claims to be a reading, an interpretation, rather than a mere reproduction. Deconstruction is not indebted to the gift of the signifier, of representation, to which it is thereby bound to serve. It is indebted to the withdrawal of the signifier, to the excess without sign, one much like the difference between marrano and Jew, which is secret not because lost or unknown, but because unsigned and/or forged. The subject of deconstruction is not language, for deconstruction is an agent, an *instance* (in French, *instance* means "instant" and "agent") of language.

In "Abraham" Derrida says that "I play seriously, more and more, with the figure of the marrano." Derrida thus includes marrano among all the other figures that he casts as irreducible to the signifier: pharmakon, writing, différance, *revenant*, specter, rogue, trace, gap, aporia, and many others. Derrida continually alters his head signifiers for two reasons: (a) The shifting from one to another signifier, *even if they mean the same*, opens distinct fields, as pharmakon sparks an alteration in the reading of Plato's mimesis/eidos dialectic, whereas *revenant* or specter stimulates novel interventions into Marx and Shakespeare, and (b) because Derrida does not want any one signifier to serve as a model for deconstruction, exemplify the deconstructive operation. Hence, it is not surprising that Derrida points up, in "Abraham, the Other," twenty or so words for Jew, including marrano. Like difference, writing, pharmakon, Derrida's "marrano" is a repetition of other deconstructive gestures that concern repetition. In order to save the "deconstruction" of the Jew from slipping into the mire over which it founders, that is, into the transcendental signifier that allows the meaning of man, human meaning, order, to arise—the Jew as model of modern or alienated man who is indebted to the Other and thus, as example or ideal, "does not exist" in actuality, hence can be sacrificed—Derrida supplements his Jew with other Judeities, each repeating and displacing the other: Marrano supplements Jew; Jew supplements pharmakon; pharmakon supplements writing; writing supplements supplement. If the Jew is the example of the being that is most itself for *not* enjoying the quality of an itself, then the marrano cannot be a sharper example of that phenomenon, more Jew than the Jew, but can only add one more deconstructive example, serve as yet another idiotic supplement that exposes the human, and metaphysics, to their difference from themselves, which scares them to death: scares them, unfortunately, to reconstructing signifiers—migrant, dealer, terrorist, even marrano—that embody death, since it is because death is not a signifier, not an identifiable sign, that it frightens so.

When Derrida, for example, follows Plato's naming of writing as *pharmakon* in "Plato's Pharmacy," he initiates a discussion about biopolitics that no endeavor after 9/11 can ignore. In the wake of *pharmakon*, terror, immunity, scapegoating, and event are never to be the same. Such is the case with all Derridean nonsigns. Each inserts Derrida into a distinct situation, altering that situation, a situation that otherwise does not exist, so as to redisclose it on deconstruction's terms, which terms Derrida then places under erasure, beginning again. Derrida, therefore, would "play. . . .with the figure of the marrano," offering still another example of the Jew, only if he could make the marrano *play* a role that "Jew" cannot, a feat he accomplishes in two ways: (1) He, Derrida, inserts himself as alien into the Hispanic idiom (*marrano* is a Spanish word, even when used in other languages), and that idiom, the idiom of the Spanish and Hispanism, into an alien project, that of the marrano Derrida, the discourse of deconstruction; and (2) he adds *play*, that which is not useful, not justified, possesses no reason, into the question of race and racism, neither of which is—no race is, and no racism is—for a reason, or "with reason."

Derrida's "operation marrano," by extension, thus says important things to Latin Americanism, the discourse in which I work, and one of the chief dwelling place of marranos. It says first that, insofar as Latin Americanism conceives deconstruction as an example of thought, of universal thought that represents or fails to represent the particular content of Latin America, Latin Americanism remains, in the age of theory, what it has been since it began: a return to philology. For the name of the conflict between theory as a form of thinking and Latin America as the content to be thought, is, precisely, philology, whose other name is patriarchy: patriarchy or ideology. Second, between the Other who calls Latin America "Latin America," and the Latin Americans who call themselves themselves—between, metaphorically, "I, a Jew" and "Jew eat"—falls neither sameness nor difference but the compulsion to repeat, idiocy, the death drive, the opening to the risk that these same distinctions, within Latin Americanism, are deployed as means to eliminate (eliminate opening, danger) in the name of identity. And third, which third repeats the first and second, Derrida's marranismo illustrates that a universal such as Eurocentrism does not deny the particular, such as Latin America, but is its requisite, so that any claim on particularity as alterity is an embrace of the *père*, of the exemplarity of the universal, hence of Eurocentrism as such. It is the maintenance of nationalism via localism. Latin Americanism, alleging its significance as a different identity or a set of different signifiers/subjects, can display only its epiphenomenal redundancy. Here, we might remind those who insist that, without subject, no politics is possible, that before the subject can be political, it must, by logical necessity, be meaningful. Latin Americanism's demand for politics is for a significant, universally exemplary subject: a father and master signifier, recognized by itself and its others. Efforts to save the discipline by rescuing it from "theory" or, for that matter, literature (in the name of the age-old, but still good "let us go back into the streets"), stand as mad rushes to pave a proper, humanist, signed, identifiable way upon the road map of the planning processes that, within our universities, patiently and effectively plot either the obsolescence of the humanities and of Latin Americanism, or worse.

NOTES

1. See my discussion of this matter in "Management of the Estate in *La verdad sospechosa*," 166–68.

2. I am of course referring to the Parisian students who, in 1968, defended their leader Daniel Cohn-Bendit, who had been accused by the authorities of being a foreigner (Cohn-Bendit, born in France, had German Jewish parents), by adopting the slogan "We are all German Jews."

WORKS CITED

Borges, Jorge Luis. "I, a Jew." In *Selected Non-Fictions*, edited by Eliot Weinberger, 110–11. New York: Penguin, 1999.

de Man, Paul. *The Resistance to Theory*. Minneapolis: University of Minnesota Press, 1986.

Derrida, Jacques. "Abraham, the Other." In *Judeities: Questions for Jacques Derrida*, translated by Bettina Bergo and Michael B. Smith, 1–35. New York: Fordham University Press, 2007.

———. *Dissemination*. Translated by Barbara Johnson. Chicago: University of Chicago Press, 1981.

Lacan, Jacques. *Le Seminaire, Livre XIX . . . ou pire*. Paris: Champ Freudien, 2011.

———. *The Seminar. Book XX, Encore, on Feminine Sexuality: The Limits of Love and Knowledge*. Translated by Bruce Fink. New York: W. W. Norton, 1998.

Levinson, Brett. "The Management of the Estate in *La verdad sospechosa*." *Revista de Estudios Hispánicos* 28, no. 2 (1994): 163–84.

Sartre, Jean Paul. *Anti-Semite and Jew: An Exploration of the Etiology of Hate*. Translated by Michael Walzer. New York: Schocken Books, 1948. Print.

Žižek, Slavoj. "It Doesn't Have to Be a Jew." Interview by Josefina Ayerza. *Lusitania* 1, no. 4 (1994).

CHAPTER 5

Two Sides of the Same Coin?
Form, Matter, and Secrecy in Derrida, de Man, and Borges

Patrick Dove

According to the *Diccionario de la Real Academia Española* the term "marrano" derives from the Arabic *muḥarram*, which means "forbidden" or "anathematized" and presumably alludes to Muslim and Jewish proscriptions against eating pork. *Marrano* made its way into colloquial Spanish with the meaning of "pig" or "pork" and later acquired an array of derogatory cultural associations including "a Jew who has converted to Catholicism but who covertly practices Judaism," and more generally "an accursed, wicked or nefarious person," "a dirty, grubby person," "a rude person with no manners," and "someone who acts badly or in a low manner." Only in the first meaning is the connection between animality and presumed concealment of a forbidden religious and/or cultural difference explicitly present; in the others the motif of a secret whose content has been determined as illicit or improper finds itself transcoded into an aesthetic language in which wickedness, dirtiness, and baseness hold the place of a moral fault that dare not speak its true name.

In "History of the Lie" Derrida links the figure of the marrano to a dephenomenalization of the secret. The "difference" named by the marrano could no longer be explained through the calculus of cultural or religious identities. Beyond whatever determinable and demonstrable cultural or religious difference might be found in this figure, the marrano gives shadowy form to what Derrida calls an "absolute secret" whose paradoxical structure requires some elaboration. This secret does not hide anything, or at least it need not hide anything in order to constitute a secret. The thought of an "absolute secret" whose structure precludes any possible disclosure pushes back against a powerful structure of confessional demands that, throughout the history of Western modernity, have required that certain people declare—in front of others and in front of power—who they are, including and especially their secrets. The "absolute secret" of the marrano pushes back not just against the confessional discourse of power and its institutions but also against restitutive operations that equate the act of giving voice to alternative identities with justice.

Moving against the grain of a powerful phenomenalism that would define the public or political sphere as a space of unmediated transparency the marrano insists, at the very limits of phenomenal referentiality, on an inalienable right to secrecy or silence: secrecy as prior to and irreducible to any identitarian position or content, prior to and irreducible to any ipseity or *whatness* of a subject. The marrano acts as a restrainer against what Derrida describes as the "absolute hegemony of political reason [and] a limitless extension of the region of the political" (Derrida, "History of the Lie," 63), against a hegemonic logic that includes both the history of nationalisms with their fetishistic quests for cultural and biological "purity" and the history of redemptive identitarian emancipations of those who have been excluded by nationalist projects. The marrano secret insists on a limit for the state and its representational mandate, and more generally for what, following Derrida, we might call politicism understood as the tendency to equate the political with the entirety or essence of the social. In marking a limit for politicist totalization, moreover, the marrano may in fact also preserve the possibility for politics as such, assuming that one accepts that politics begins when a limit is drawn for the hegemony of state reason, or when a crack opens up in the edifice of hegemonic reason. In this sense it belongs to the register that Alberto Moreiras calls the infrapolitical as an affirmation of the irreducibility of the social to any political totalization (Moreiras, "Literatura infrapolítica"). The marrano secret might be thought of as analogous to what Thoreau calls "civil disobedience": an inalienable right to act in the public sphere that cannot be legislated, codified, or guaranteed by any constitutional law, precisely because it names a right to disregard or transgress the law under special circumstances that obtain when reasoned reflection brings one to the conclusion that the law in question must be disobeyed in the name of a higher law, or even in the name of the underlying principle of the law itself. The marrano secret, as envisioned by Derrida, would therefore have no positive content. It would not keep anything phenomenal from the law, it would keep only the law's imperial tendency to extend itself over the entirety of the social.

As Erin Graff Zivin has pointed out, Derrida's association of the marrano with a "formal" secrecy—or a secret devoid of phenomenal content—cuts against ontotheological determinations of truth according to the structure of revelation. The marrano secret, if there is one, would be irreducible to any metaphysical opposition between essence and appearance, veiling and unveiling, dissimulation and revelation, forgetting and remembering, and so on. For Graff Zivin the association of the marrano with a form of secrecy that resists phenomenalization also responds to a history of material practices of power through which the kind of radical heterogeneity named by the marrano has been targeted by state power and subjected to the tactics and technologies designed to make people speak. It would seem that what hegemonic reason cannot abide is the possibility of a "marrano difference" that would be irreducible to ontological distinctions between identity and difference, proper and improper, us and them. The marrano presents state reason and its absolute distinctions with a problem that must be made to disappear—precisely by compelling it to speak its name. The principal object of inquisitional practice, Graff Zivin proposes, is not to procure information but to compel the other to show itself and to take a stand within the field of the revealable: as either *this* or *that*, Jewish or Catholic, one of us or outsider, friend or foe, and so on. What must be eliminated or expelled, accordingly, is not the other qua calculable difference (the Jew, the outsider, the enemy) but anything that does not comply with the phenomenalizing demands of hegemonic reason: Show yourself, speak your name!

In what follows I propose that the thematization of a "marrano Derrida" could be said to hold the place of a series of elisions, suppressions, secrets, and expulsions that may be impossible fully to enumerate. The focus on a "marrano Derrida" may also be difficult to separate—but separate it we must!—from a tendency to overestimate the later work of Derrida and its focus on ethical and political concerns while concurrently disregarding earlier confrontations with philosophical and linguistic problems. Taking up the works of the "later Derrida" could allow us to feel more comfortable in abandoning the earlier works and thereby avoiding some of their defining preoccupations: the rigorous dismantling of logocentrism, alongside the careful demonstration that in an important sense we have not yet begun to read the canonical works of Plato, Rousseau, Kant, Hegel, Freud, Heidegger, and many others.

The enthusiastic reception of the "later Derrida" in contemporary academic conversations is, as a general phenomenon, anything but innocent or neutral. It sustains an unspoken effort to save deconstruction, or theory in general, from itself in at least two ways. The ethicopolitical turn in deconstruction provides readers of Derrida with an opportunity to change focus following disclosures of scandalous political associations and statements associated with the names of Martin Heidegger and Paul de Man. The turn to ethics and politics could also be said to mobilize a splitting within deconstruction itself, between one tendency that continues to come back to questions about language, rhetoric, and text, and another that has now moved beyond those concerns in favor of what are called "real-world problems." This turn provides a reassuring response to those who would equate deconstruction with the undermining of truth, morality, or reality itself. Deconstruction, we now see, can do more than just call into question and destabilize accepted and self-evident truths: It also provides critical tools for combating racism, the death penalty, nuclear proliferation, terrorism, and other perils associated with unrestrained state power. But if the ethical and political Derrida is welcomed based on a promise to redeem deconstruction as critical practice, by way of provocation I propose the following question: To what extent are the academic welcoming of a "later Derrida," on the one hand, and efforts to delegitimize deconstruction through ad hominem attacks and blatant misreading, on the other, in fact two sides of the same coin?

When we equate "Derrida" or "deconstruction" with the figure of the marrano, could it be that we unwittingly run the risk of sanctioning an ongoing expulsion of certain disruptive, unsettling, heterogeneous effects associated with the critical practice of deconstruction? In raising this question I do not mean to suggest that we should *not* speak of a "marrano" Derrida or that we should ignore the turn to ethical and political themes, as if in doing so we could or should want to safeguard a "pure" form of deconstruction uncontaminated by external factors. But in the very act of asserting, against those who would dismiss it altogether, that deconstruction really does possess a political or ethical efficacy, are we unintentionally accommodating and further legitimizing the technicist, instrumental demands made on us by the corporate university, demands that require that all time be accounted for and that all investments be explained and justified ahead of time in instrumental terms? Under such conditions, what if we were to declare that there is no such thing as a "marrano specter"? What if, in welcoming the specter of the marrano into the conversation, one is either already too marrano or still not marrano enough?

It may be that the only "marrano" remaining—if there is one—is whatever it is that continues to insist and call out to us today under the name of that other deconstructive thinker, Paul de Man. I mean both a de Man whose tendential expulsion from contemporary critical conversations coincides with a massive depreciation of critical attention to questions about language and thought, and a de Man whose work has never received anything more than a very limited treatment within rank-and-file Hispanism.[1] Even more so than the potential blind spots that arise when we try to distinguish between an "earlier" and a "later" Derrida, the expulsion of de Man from contemporary conversations about deconstruction is symptomatic of something that ought to be interrogated in the light of day. It attests once again to a perceived need to save deconstruction, not only from the ethical and political lapses committed by some of its practitioners, and not only from the baseless and thoughtless association of deconstruction with relativism or nihilism. The expulsion of de Man is indicative of a need to purge deconstruction of its concern for language as such, or at least from a certain way of thinking language that de Man associates with "materiality."

To be fair and accurate, de Man has not been completely expelled from contemporary theoretical discussions, nor has what I am calling his tendential expulsion from deconstruction gone unnoticed. Among recent discussions of de Man and his legacy in deconstructive circles, some of the most provocative are a 2001 volume titled *Material Events: Paul de Man and the Afterlife of Theory*, coedited by Tom Cohen, Barbara Cohen, J. Hillis Miller, and Andrzej Warminski (the volume explores understudied aspects of de Man's posthumously published *Aesthetic Ideology* and its surprising emphasis on "materiality" and "material history"); more recent essays by Cohen ("Toxic Assets" and "De Man vs. 'Deconstruction'"), as well as a pair of 2013 monographs by Warminski (*Material Inscriptions* and *Ideology, Rhetoric, Aesthetics*). As we will see later, one of Warminski's great merits is to have shown how the concerns raised in de Man's late turn to "material history," and which provide the focal point for the *Material Events* contributions, were in fact already at work in earlier writings on Hölderlin, Rousseau, and Nietzsche from the late 1960s and '70s. Warminski thereby deals a decisive blow against any possibility of constructing a progressive chronological account of de Man's work: from rhetoric to the real, from text to history, etc. Although these studies make important contributions to advancing our understanding of de Man's work, they do not entirely

resolve the underlying question that I am interested in pursuing here. If
the expulsion of de Man can be perceived as either an overly hasty com-
pensation or as an ideologically motivated attempt to "purify" deconstruction of an ailment that has been afflicting it—and for which de Man would
be the metonymical or catachrestic stand-in—what then would it mean
to call de Man back or to call for his reinstatement? On what grounds
can one today assert that de Man has been unjustly or unduly expelled
and that he should therefore be brought back? Is this because we believe
that de Man's peculiar methodology of reading could be useful in dealing
with new problems confronting the world today? Is utility the measure by
which de Man is to be brought back? Or do we want to claim that de Man
is still relevant today because his work and his method can help defend the
humanities and literary studies at a time when both are faring badly in the
world? Regardless of which rationale one chooses, there will be a trap that
is difficult to avoid: Either one instrumentalizes a form of thought that
relentlessly resists instrumentalization or one unapologetically ideologizes
(in the sense that de Man gives to the term in his essay on Kant and Schiller) a form of thought that was relentless in its efforts to call attention to
the difference between ideology and history. Although there may not be
any surefire way of avoiding such pitfalls, de Man's work does teach us that
there are different ways of approaching them. If there is no way of avoiding
ideology altogether, that does not necessarily mean that everything is pure
ideology, nor does it dictate that we should simply embrace ideology in our
own thinking and critical practices.

In *Aesthetic Ideology*, in his reading of Kant and Hegel and their respec-
tive discussions of the sublime, de Man insists on a fundamental, unsur-
passable distinction between what he calls "history" and "ideology." To
history, he says, pertains what actually happens, whereas ideology arises
through the conflation of reference and phenomenalism, or with the assimilation of what actually happens back into sequential, chronological
narratives of purpose, progress, and unification. However we characterize
its occurrence, ideology generates a perspective from which heterogeneity is calculated as difference, and occurrences in their singularity are re-
absorbed within narratives of continuity. Ideology is a refusal of the event
understood as occurrence that punctures or disrupts a prevailing horizon
of sense.

De Man illustrates the distinction between history and ideology by
pointing to a discrepancy between Kant's account of aesthetic experience
in the third *Critique* and Schiller's appropriation of Kantian conceptual vo-
cabulary in his *On the Aesthetic Education of Man*. Schiller mobilizes and in-

strumentalizes the Kantian account of the aesthetic for a nonphilosophical goal: that of securing a stable site from which conflict and discord can be reconciled and replaced by harmonious totalities (subjects, nations). Schiller puts the aesthetic to work as a space for molding responsible citizens in democratic societies: citizens who will work for freedom while knowing how to avoid the fatal attractions of political passion. The ideological nature of Schiller's use of Kant can best be appreciated, however, when we return to Kant and begin to ask exactly what Schiller might be turning away from in his appropriation of the third *Critique*. De Man uncovers in Kant's text an unsettling account of aesthetic activity that cannot be brought back into the fold of any redemptive understanding of what art is, of what it might be capable of doing or saying to us. What Kant has to say about the sublime has the potential—for those willing to read—to call into question the entire framework of modern aesthetic theory. In contrast to Schiller's account of the aesthetic as ideal pedagogical space for modern, democratic societies, Kant presents what de Man describes as a "formal materialism that runs counter to all values and characteristics associated with aesthetic experience, including the aesthetic experience of the beautiful and of the sublime as described by Kant and Hegel themselves" (de Man, *Aesthetic Ideology*, 136). De Man locates the emergence of this seemingly self-contradictory idea of "formal materialism" in the "General Comment" of the third *Critique*, which immediately follows Kant's distinction between mathematical and analytic sublime. It arises specifically in the description of poetic vision as an encounter with a flattened-out world in which objects have been stripped bare of any depth or any anthropocentrically determined meaning or purpose. "Formal materialism" obtains with the vision of a radically dehumanized sky as seen by the poet, as a "vast vault" that provides no shelter for dwelling and no promise of eternal life, or of the ocean when seen as a "clear mirror of water bounded only by the sky" that sustains no thought of depth or abundance (Kant, *Critique of Judgment*, 130). As we will see, this strange and estranging Kantian aesthetic vision of the world will become, in de Man's hands, an allegory of language itself.

The association of Kant's aesthetic vision with a world freed from any and all subjective valuations is perfectly clear: In the third *Critique* Kant goes to great lengths to demonstrate that an *aesthetic* judgment of taste must happen separately from any and all "pathological" interest, that is, ideas about the utility, value, or meaning of an object. It is form and not content that determines the aesthetic quality of the object. But why "materiality"? The only explanation offered by de Man is an enigmatic one: "Material vision is the only word that comes to mind" (de Man, *Aesthetic Ideology*, 82).

One could surmise that materiality plays a role analogous to that of "resistance" in the "Resistance to Theory" essay (de Man, *Resistance to Theory*), one of whose possible referents is matter as the stuff of physical reality, insofar as its resistance to perception and cognition is both a limit and a condition of possibility for any experience or knowledge of the world. Like the dove in Kant's first *Critique*, thought cannot hope to make headway in the world except in relation to the resistance offered by the real in its materiality. What de Man calls material history happens where tropological operations fail to work as they ought to; they do not produce cognition and understanding but instead leave a nonnegatable ("material") remainder or residue for reading.

De Man's curious pseudo-explanation, that material vision is "the only word that comes to mind," also cannot help but recall his commentaries on Rousseau in *Allegories of Reading*, especially his reading of Rousseau's famous "confession" of theft. As a young boy, Rousseau recalls, he was employed in the house of an aristocratic family. One day he stole a ribbon belonging to a female employee, and, when the purloined object was discovered, he quickly blamed a female servant by the name of Marion. He adds that he was infatuated with Marion and that he had planned to give the ribbon to her as a gift. The odd element in Rousseau's account, of course, is his explanation for why, when confronted about the stolen ribbon, he would blame precisely the person to whom he was planning to give the ribbon. Rousseau writes that he "excused [himself] on the first object that presented itself" (as quoted in de Man, *Allegories of Reading*, 288): as if the name "Marion" were a thing upon which he could lean for support ("excuse himself *on*"), and as if the name had decided *to give itself to him* in the manner of an automaton. For de Man, Rousseau's strange confessional account produces a vision of the machine-like workings of the signifier; it thereby announces the possibility of what he describes as "an entirely different system in which terms such as desire, shame, guilt, exposure, and repression no longer have any place," a nonhuman, technical or mechanical system at the heart of what we continue to think of as human language (289). Materiality for de Man names an effort to think language beyond humanist accounts, to think language as irreducible to any attribute of a subject: consciousness, will, intention, and so on. It attempts to think language as a machine that produces effects independent of whatever the speaking subject might mean to say. "There can be no use of language," writes de Man, "which is not, within a certain perspective thus radically formal, i.e., mechanical, no matter how deeply this aspect may be concealed by aesthetic, formalistic delusions" (294). Here we see that as early as 1979 de Man was already proposing a surprising association of "formalism" with "materiality."

In "Typewriter Ribbon" Jacques Derrida provides both a fascinating meditation on what it would mean to think machine and event together, and an extensive critique of de Man's rhetorical reading of Rousseau. One of the major critical claims made by Derrida is that de Man, in trying to distinguish between "confession" and "excuse" in Rousseau's discourse, relies on an all-too-clear and stable distinction between constative and performative modes of discourse, when in fact Rousseau's text shows that the confessional mode contains a fold in which describing and doing would prove to be interwoven in undecidable fashion. However, it seems to me that a careful reading of *Allegories of Reading* would find that Derrida's criticisms have already been anticipated in de Man's reading and that the object of critique is therefore nothing other than an average reading that mistakenly assumes that de Man privileges the performative speech act over its constative counterpart—as if one could have text as act while bypassing the tropological system as it reconstructs itself for understanding. De Man, meanwhile, is fully aware that one cannot have the one without the other: There is no critique of tropology that does not reproduce the very system it criticizes, no critique of ideology that does not also reproduce or enable the conflation of reference and phenomenalism. By the same token if de Man privileges anything in his attention to materiality it is not the performative but the passage as such from one modality of language to another.

The linguistic model for what de Man calls material history is to be found in "the passage from trope, which is a cognitive model, to the performative, for example" (de Man, *Aesthetic Ideology*, 132). It is not the performative itself, as some readers have too hastily concluded, but *the passage as such* from a nominally closed cognitive system of tropes to another system and another conception of language—a performative language of power—whose workings cannot be comprehended or explained from within the system of cognition. In the posthumous *Aesthetic Ideology* essays de Man focuses primarily on the movement from tropological to performative uses of language to illustrate what this strange thought of formal materiality would look like: an irreversible transfer or shift from one domain to another whose occurrence cannot be explained using the logical and chronological models of epistemology. This shift or movement between modalities leaves us within language—materiality is not outside of language for de Man—while making it very difficult to say *what* language is. The passage from one modality to another illuminates a fold within the fabric of language whose traversal can never be undone: Once we have crossed the line—for instance, from a language of cognition to a language of power—we can never return to cognition in order to grasp what has transpired. Or, more precisely, in trying to return from a language of power to a language of cognition, we abandon materiality in favor of ideology. The material passage may be akin to what Friedrich Hölderlin tried to think as caesura: a turn that ensures that beginning and end, before and after, can never be made to rhyme.

Elsewhere in de Man's writings one finds similar irreversible turns in juxtapositions between other modalities of language: between grammar and rhetoric (the famous "Archie Bunker" episode); between trope and anthropomorphism (as in the reading of Nietzsche's discussion of truth in *Allegories of Reading*); and so on. In all cases, history, by which de Man understands "what actually happens" as the passage in between modalities, must be distinguished from any chronological process. What happens in and as history is not even temporal in nature. Whenever and wherever something happens, it does so as a spark or lightning bolt that crosses the gap between systems or modalities of inscription: of cognition and power, description and promise, and so on. Once temporal sequencing begins its work, meanwhile, we unavoidably find ourselves in the realm of ideology in which reference and tropology are mistaken for phenomenalism. Again, this lapse back into ideology should not be mistaken for a traditional understanding of ideology as false consciousness. The slippage into ideology cannot be avoided, just as there can be no thinking outside of the language of chronologization and cognition. For this reason we can never be satisfied with simply unmasking or demystifying tropological systems, and deconstruction as de Man practices it should not be confused with a critical practice of unmasking forms of deception. As de Man never tires of demonstrating, the critique of tropology is unable to have done with tropes once and for all. Critique invariably ends up substituting one trope for another, even if this means substituting a "trope of the literal" (real, true, demystified, critical) for a "trope of the figural" (fictive, false, mystified, uncritical).

As Andrzej Warminski has shown, de Man's concerns with the distinction between history and ideology can be traced back as far as the 1967 Gauss lectures, and specifically to his criticism of Heidegger's reading of Hölderlin's "Wie wenn am Feiertage." There de Man takes issue with what he sees as Heidegger's tendency to ignore patterns of temporal reversal in the poetic text while imposing a Hegelian forward-oriented understanding of history. When he pushes back against progressive accounts of de Man's work (e.g., from rhetoric to materiality), it turns out that Warminski is also reading de Man against himself. In the preface to *Allegories of Reading* de Man confesses that the project was unable to complete what it set out to accomplish: a historical study of Romanticism. Had it been realized, however, the historical project would have been anything but historical in the sense de Man will give to this term in the *Aesthetic Ideology* essays. In reading Rousseau, de Man recounts, he found himself unable to progress beyond what he calls "local difficulties of interpretation" and was therefore obliged to abandon the historicist project of tracing lines of literary influence and evolution in favor of what he calls "the problematics of reading" (ix). This self-described shift from history to reading has been taken by some readers as confirmation of the limitations of de Man's methodologies, of a way of reading that characteristically proves incapable of dealing with real-world problems ("history") and turns instead to the solipsistic realm of textual interpretation. But, as Warminski notes, such readers may be a little too comfortable in their presumed knowledge of what de Man understands by "the problematics of reading." As the essays in *Allegories of Reading* illustrate, the shift from the goal of producing a historical account of Romanticism to the problem of reading is in fact already a move *past* the tropological structures of rhetoric and *into* the disjunctive torsion of intersystemic passages that will later give rise to the strange term "formal materialism." The move from historicism to reading is always already a move past rhetoric and toward an awareness that tropological textual models are unable to account for what actually happens in and as the texts of Hölderlin, Wordsworth, Rousseau, and others (Warminski, *Ideology, Rhetoric, Aesthetics*, 182).

If Paul de Man names metonymically what had to be left out so that deconstruction could be reconstituted in the wake of the scandalous "affairs" of the 1980s and during subsequent decades in the context of an increasingly corporatized university defined by the calculative logic of accountability and practical applications, the point of conjuring up de Man once again is not because a simple return to close reading and rhetorical analysis would be preferable to engagement with political or ethical texts and contexts. It is not a question of choosing one or the other. It is because what de Man names metonymically also turns out to belong to the historical self-definition of the humanities in which all of us work: as a general field of study concerned with questions about language, symbolic production, translation, and the conditions that make thought and understanding possible in the first place. To dismiss de Man because it is not clear how one can get from rhetorical reading to the spheres of political action or ethical praxis—and the transition is admittedly not always easy to see—

would be to reproduce an ideological regression that acknowledges only
that which can be subsumed without remainder in a sequential order of
purposes, causes, and effects. If, on the contrary, we are seeking footholds
from which to think history without reducing it to developmentalist tele-
ology, de Man's rhetorical readings with their attention to the disjunctive
character of what actually happens may well provide some much-needed
new light. If de Man's thought can still play a significant role in the humanities today, moreover, its significance for us today may turn out to be linked
to the way in which his readings resist easy assimilation into rationales of
utility and transparency. The writing off of de Man, in this sense, names
metonymically a refusal of the discomfort that we experience in the face
of refractoriness or resistance. And, as de Man has taught us better than
perhaps anyone, it is precisely in relation to such resistance that thinking
itself takes flight.

In the *Aesthetic Ideology* essays and in work presented at the same time—
such as the essay on Benjamin's "Task of the Translator"—de Man returns
frequently to a thought of language that would not be definable in human
terms or recuperable as the proper domain of the subject. "The principle
of closure," de Man says in the "Kant and Schiller" essay, "is not the human—because language can always undo that principle of closure—and
[it] is not language either, because language is not a firm concept, is not a
concept of an entity which allows itself to be conceptualized and reified in
any way" (de Man, *Aesthetic Ideology*, 151–52). That we don't have a concept that would be adequate for thinking what we call "language" presents
the reverse side of the coin to de Man's infamous assertion that "*death* is
a displaced name for a *linguistic predicament*" (de Man, *Rhetoric of Romanticism*, 81). If what we call death is in fact a catachresis or improper name
for a problem having to do with language, then language cannot possibly
be synonymous with the discursive or rhetorical domain to which de Man
is often accused of reducing everything that is not trope or figure. But,
of course, we cannot simply separate language from the tropological either. Thus, for de Man, language is not a self-contained system or even
a phenomenon. It is a condition of splitting or being split, a turnstile of
sorts that is continuously placing us over on the other side from where we
thought we were. And, to be perfectly clear, it is we who are split in this
way by language. Although we can only ever think and act from within
language, we can never simply and properly be within the split. If death is
a displaced name for a linguistic predicament, this linguistic predicament
is in turn an experience of displacement that both marks us as speaking and

thinking beings while ruining any possibility of achieving full mastery of our existence or our words.

I now turn to a short text by Jorge Luis Borges, first published in the Argentine daily *La nación* in 1950, titled "La muralla y los libros." The essay offers a meditation on the Emperor Shi Huang Ti, also known as Qin Shi Huang (literally, "the first Emperor of Qin"), whose political activities suggest to Borges a way of thinking about aesthetic experience. Shi Huang was the king of the state of Qin; in 221 BC he put an end to regional conflict between feudal lords (the "Warring States") and presided over the unification of China, of which he then became the first emperor. Borges focuses on two remarkable feats commonly associated with the Qin dynasty: the construction of an immense wall encompassing the new territory in its entirety; and a decree calling for the burning of all previously existing books in the empire. These two vast operations together constitute what Borges calls the mythical dimension of the imperial dynasty. Taken together, as construction and destruction on a scale that almost exceeds all measure, they constitute an enigma that Borges finds at once disturbing and strangely satisfying.

"La muralla y los libros" unfolds as an investigation into the source and implications of these competing tendencies. What matters is not the historical accuracy (or lack thereof) of the feats attributed to Shi Huang but their formal arrangement, the way in which the attributed deeds fit together as two mutually complementary sides of a narrative of origins. The essay entertains a series of possible motives for these two expenditures of power and labor. First, Borges proposes a political explanation that he attributes to "certain sinologists." Both endeavors, according to some scholars, belong to the same practice of power. In space Shi Huang Ti shows himself to be the author of an enclosure that serves to demarcate the space of the proper while securing its borders against the threat of invasion. Order in this account would be derived in a Hobbesian manner: from a production of space that simultaneously casts the threat of disorder (the old conflict between Warring States) outside, where it is reconfigured as the specter of barbarian invasion. Operating in the realm of time, meanwhile, the emperor mandates the wholesale destruction of the past together with its images and forms of knowledge. He thereby deprives his political opponents of a vast archive of alternatives to the present order while establishing his rule as the true, undivided origin of all history. The two gestures, ostensibly antithetical, together constitute the complementary sides of imperial command and reason: space and time, production and destruction,

inscription and proscription. Construction and annihilation are the do-
mains of princes, this account concludes, and the only unusual feature in
Shi Huang Ti's story is the colossal scale of the endeavor.

The essay then goes on to consider several other hypotheses, each of
which discovers an ironic symmetry between the two operations. Enclosure and book burning are ritual acts with a common goal: to ward
off death. Or the wall is a tutelary metaphor: Those who have been con-
demned to a life of hard labor erecting it are the same political opponents
who formerly praised the rulers described in the books of old, presenting
them as desirable alternatives to the current ruler; their toiling away at
such a grandiose enterprise metaphorizes for all the folly of dissidence. According to another hypothesis, Shi Huang ordered the construction of the
wall after envisioning a future prince who will one day decide to take over
the first emperor's place in history; but in ordering the destruction of the
monumental wall this usurper will in fact unwittingly become the double
of Shi Huang. There is no negation that does not repeat or become that
which it destroys.

The short essay culminates by affirming in the anecdote about Shi
Huang something that Kant would call aesthetic judgment. The strange
appeal that this fable holds for us is owing, Borges insists, to its form alone.
The interest or unease it provokes in us has nothing to do with the possible motives or hidden meanings that we might attribute to it.[2] Akin to
the Kantian account of the beautiful, the operations ordered by Huang
Ti are striking precisely insofar as they do not harbor any (conjectural)
conceptual content.

> The tenacious wall which at this moment, and at all moments, casts
> its system of shadows over lands I shall never see, is the shadow of a
> Caesar who ordered the most reverent of all nations to burn its past; it
> is plausible that this idea moves us in itself, aside from the conjectures
> it allows. . . . Generalizing from the preceding case, we could infer that
> all forms have their virtue in themselves and not in any conjectural
> "content." (Borges, "The Wall and the Books," 188)

We should not conclude too hastily, however, that Borges has contented
himself with producing a literary confirmation of a formalist aesthetic according to which the essence of art lies beyond the concept and that all
conceptual labor and analysis is therefore antithetical to authentic appre-
ciation. Aesthetic experience happens prior to the understanding, true, but
art and concept are not for that reason simply opposed. If it is form alone

that generates interest, this is because aesthetic experience properly attends to the taking place of form itself, the cognitive grasping of formal unity from out of the chaotic manifold of experience. Although the aesthetic effect presupposes the suspension of all "conjectural content" (concepts of use, meaning, value, etc.), it should be clear that there can be no conceptuality without the aesthetic understood as taking place of form: no reason and no action, no ethics and no politics in the absence of our capacity to grasp form ("the People," "class," "Latin America," and so on).

At first glance the proposed generalization of this fable ("generalizando el caso anterior") may appear to yield somewhat disappointing results. It seems to leave us comfortably within what de Man would call Schillerian aesthetic ideology, or a determination of aesthetic experience as providing a model for the state as tutelary model for the modern citizen and as mediator of conflict and discord. There is nothing especially radical, philosophically or politically speaking, about the formalism that Borges appears to be advocating. But then again maybe things are not as simple as first meets the eye. In the concluding sentence we encounter a thought that throws everything up in the air again:

> Music, states of happiness, mythology, faces belabored by time, certain twilights and certain places try to tell us something, or have said something we should not have missed, or are about to say something; this imminence of a revelation which does not occur is, perhaps, the aesthetic phenomenon. (Borges, "The Wall and the Books," 188)

What Borges calls the aesthetic act turns out to depend neither on representation (e.g., the Kantian beautiful as free, harmonious play of the faculties of perception, or the Hegelian sensible representation of the absolute) nor on absence or failure (e.g., the Kantian sublime as predicated on the inability of the imagination to gather the manifold into a formal unity). Aesthetic experience obtains with the imminence of something that does not show itself, the proximity of a disclosure that does not take place. As Alberto Moreiras has shown, Borges's account of the aesthetic marks a limit for representation while avoiding the kinds of dualism that arise when one equates such limits with a nominal reality prior to representation or with something beyond representation (a precritical notion of the real). The aesthetic for Borges names an impossibility that haunts all representation from within: the thought of a revelation that would reveal what revelation itself destroys. It attributes to art or to literature the task of approaching something akin to what Heidegger calls the ontological difference, or the traces of a retreat or withdrawal that occurs alongside the presentation of what *is*. Neither immanence nor transcendence, this (non)revelation that announces itself to us as imminent, proximate, is the trace of the impossible real that inscribes itself in all representation.

By way of conclusion I want to pursue my reading of the final sentence of Borges's essay a few steps further in order to see how it sheds light on the essay in its entirety. In the process I will also bring the discussion back to de Man and "formal materialism" in a way that might help make clear how that concept (if that is what it is) might be able to speak to us today. I begin by recalling a suggestion made earlier in Borges's essay that the double operation possesses a metaphorical structure: the wall as concretization of the true meaning of dissidence, that is, futility or folly. Revelation, as the central axis of Borges's formulation of aesthetic activity, is similarly governed by a metaphorical structure: metaphor as the disclosure of resemblance or being among differences. The framing mechanism in which this formulation is to be found, meanwhile, speaks of the proximity of something that has not taken place, and it thus possesses the structure of metonymy: contiguity in space and deferral in time. Pushing these associations even further, the final sentence enacts a formal inversion of the proposed "metaphorical" reading. If the wall as spacing operation presents the truth of the temporal practice of dissidence (whose passion was fed by images taken from the past) in sensible, concrete form, in the last sentence of the essay it is time and not space that has the final word. However, what we find here is no longer what modernity has always understood by time: the sequential and progressive chronologization of the real (through revelation, for example). Time here turns out to be a knot of tendencies or movements that can neither be easily separated nor reduced to a single common sense: imminence and delay, arriving and holding back, appearing and withdrawing.

Borges's essay offers us something not unlike the "formal materialism" that de Man locates in Kant's discussion of the aesthetic and the sublime. "La muralla y los libros" first projects the semblance of a sustained, free engagement in the aesthetic play of juxtaposing opposites—time and space, construction and destruction, former and future rivals, and so on—only to leave us at the site of an irreversible turn. The conclusion enacts a passage from an oppositional mode of thinking characterized by a back-and-forth between time and space, to another modality in which the sense of at least one of these terms has undergone a drastic transformation. The crucial point for Borges's essay, then, is not that the rhetoric of revelation is replaced by a trope of deferral or withdrawal. What Borges is trying to think under the heading of the aesthetic and in this juxtaposition of revelation and stammering is precisely a passage from one modality to another in which the meaning or being of an element common to both ("time") undergoes irreversible transformation. It is in the passage itself and not on one side or the other that something happens, something that cannot subsequently be reduced to or explained by one modality or the other. What happens—and this is also my noninstrumental argument for why de Man still matters today—is that our accustomed understanding of time as homogeneous sequence of "nows" is destabilized by a thought of heterogeneity whose figure is found in the simultaneity of appearing and the trace of withdrawal. The discrete elements of time—past, present, future—can no longer be understood as self-contained "nows." Each and every "now" is haunted by the traces of what is no longer and what has not yet arrived, which is to say not just an array of possible futures but by a holding-back of time by time. Time cannot be reduced either to a chain of self-contained "nows" or to an uninterrupted flow of connected moments: If time *is* at all, if it has a being, it is also the movement of delay or detention through which the future in its newness is always arriving. Just as there can be no newness without repetition (to be new something must make itself recognizable to us as new), there can be no arrival without withdrawal or holding back. If no "now" can ever be the same as itself, as Borges's essay implies, if every present "now" is haunted by what is not, then the entire history of metaphysical determinations of history and historical time needs to be rethought. This necessity in turn has enormous implications for the developmentalist conceptions of time and history that have dominated Latin American political thought on both the Right and the Left since the days of Sarmiento.

NOTES

1. There are some notable exceptions to this trend, though they might not wish to be counted among rank-and-file Hispanists. See, for example, Jacques Lezra's 1991 translation of *Blindness and Insight* into Spanish, Brett Levinson's *The Ends of Literature*, Alberto Moreiras's "The Villain at the Center: Infrapolitical Borges," and Marco Dorfsman, *Heterogeneity of Being.*

2 If we think of these operations as manifestations of tyranny, or as ironically embodying both the heights of human ingenuity and the depths of human depravity, we are no longer dealing with the effects of an aesthetic judgment.

WORKS CITED

Borges, Jorge Luis. "La muralla y los libros." *Otras inquisiciones*. Madrid: Alianza, 2008.

———. "The Wall and the Books." Translated by James E. Irby, in *Labyrinths: Selected Stories and Other Writings*, edited by Donald A. Yates and James E. Irby, 186–88. New York: New Directions, 1964.

Cohen, Tom. "De Man vs. 'Deconstruction'; or, Who, Today, Speaks for the Anthropocene?" In *The Political Archive of Paul de Man: Property, Sovereignty and the Theotropic*, edited by Martin McQuillan. Edinburgh: Edinburgh University Press, 2012.

———. *Material Events: Paul de Man and the Afterlife of Theory*. Minneapolis: University of Minnesota Press, 2001.

———. "Toxic Assets: de Man's Remains and the Ecocatastrophic Imaginary (an American Fable)." In *Theory and the Disappearing Future: On de Man, On Benjamin*, edited by Tom Cohen, Claire Colebrook and J. Hillis Miller. New York: Routledge, 2012.

De Man, Paul. *Aesthetic Ideology*. Minneapolis: University of Minnesota Press, 1996.

———. *Allegories of Reading: Figural Language in Rousseau, Nietzsche, Rilke, and Proust*. New Haven: Yale University Press, 1979.

———. *The Resistance to Theory*. Minneapolis: University of Minnesota Press, 1986.

———. *The Rhetoric of Romanticism*. New York: Columbia University Press, 1984.

———. *Romanticism and Contemporary Criticism: The Gauss Seminar and Other Papers*. Baltimore: Johns Hopkins University Press, 1993.

———. *Visión y ceguera: ensayos sobre la retórica de la crítica contemporánea*. Edited and translated by Hugo Rodríguez-Vecchini and Jacques Lezra. Río Piedras: University of Puerto Rico Press, 1992.

Derrida, Jacques. "History of the Lie." In *Without Alibi*, translated by Peggy Kamuf. Stanford: Stanford University Press, 2002.

———. "Literature in Secret: An Impossible Filiation." In *The Gift of Death (Second Edition) and Literature in Secret*. Chicago: University of Chicago Press, 2007.

———. "Passions: 'An Oblique Offering.'" In *On the Name*. Stanford: Stanford University Press, 1993.

———. "This Strange Institution Called Literature." Interview with Derek Attridge. In *Acts of Literature*. New York: Routledge, 1992.

———. "Typewriter Ribbon: Limited Ink (2)." In *Without Alibi*, translated by Peggy Kamuf. Stanford: Stanford University Press, 2002.

Dorfsman, Marco. *Heterogeneity of Being: On Octavio Paz's Poetics of Similitude.* Lanham, Md.: University Press of America, 2015.

Dove, Patrick. *Literature and "Interregnum": Globalization, War, and the Crisis of Sovereignty in Latin America.* Albany: State University of New York Press, 2016.

———. "Literature and the Secret of the World: *2666*, Globalization and Global War." *CR: The New Centennial Review* 14, no. 3 (2014): 139–61.

Graff Zivin, Erin. *Figurative Inquisitions: Conversion, Torture and Truth in the Luso-Hispanic Atlantic.* Evanston, Ill.: Northwestern University Press, 2014.

Johnson, David. *Kant's Dog: On Borges, Philosophy and the Time of Translation.* Albany: State University of New York Press, 2013.

Kant, Immanuel. *Critique of Judgment.* Translated by Werner Pluhar. Indianapolis: Hackett, 1987.

Levinson, Brett. *The Ends of Literature: The Latin American "Boom" in the Neoliberal Marketplace.* Stanford: Stanford University Press, 2001.

Moreiras, Alberto. "Literatura infrapolítica: McCarthy, Marías, Borges." Web blog post. *Postsoberanía: Hacia un pensamiento de lo común.* February 3, 2014. http://postsoberania.blogspot.com/2014/02/alberto-moreiras-literatura .html.

———. "The Villain at the Center: Infrapolitical Borges." *CLCWeb: Comparative Literature and Culture* 4, no. 2 (2002). http://dx.doi.org/10.7771/ 1481–4374.1156.

Schiller, Friedrich. *On the Aesthetic Education of Man.* Translated by Reginald Snell. New Haven: Yale University Press, 1954.

Warminski, Andrzej. *Ideology, Rhetoric, Aesthetics: For de Man.* Edinburgh: Edinburgh University Press, 2013.

———. *Material Inscriptions: Rhetorical Reading in Practice and Theory.* Edinburgh: Edinburgh University Press, 2013.

PART III

Between Nonethics and Infrapolitics

CHAPTER 6

Marrano Spirit? . . . and Hispanism, or Responsibility in 2666

Gareth Williams

There's *nothing* inside the man who sits there writing.
Nothing of himself, I mean. . . . There's *nothing* in the
guts of the man who sits there writing. . . . He writes
like someone taking dictation. . . . His novel or book . . .
arises . . . as the result of an exercise of *concealment*.

—ROBERTO BOLAÑO, 2666

The following pages begin by offering a brief reflection on the conference panels that were organized by Erin Graff Zivin at the American Comparative Literature Association and the University of Southern California in 2014, under the title "The Marrano Spirit: Derrida and Hispanism." These panels were the origin of the current volume.

What remains to be said about spirit? Indeed, is there anything at all to be said about a specifically Marrano Spirit that titles our conference and brings us together with both words capitalized and without quotation marks around either of them, individually or collectively. And what can be said of the *and Hispanism* in the volume's title—of Spirit in relation to a field, to a certain form of territorialization, a sociology, and therefore in relation to a will to know and a will to power all unburdened of quotation marks? Furthermore, how to transmit what remains to be said when fidelity on either count—on the count of Spirit and of Hispanism; again, both without a hint or mark of a doubling, of a spectrality—cannot be an option, although it might also be the only condition of what brings them, and us, together? What can be the place of any decision, and therefore the place of any notion of the political, in the relation between these words and the problems they entail at first glance?

In a section of his memoir *An Impatient Life* titled "Fourth Person Singular," Daniel Bensaïd reflects on the question of fidelity and inheritance: "It is the heirs who decide the inheritance. They make the selection, and are more faithful to it in infidelity than in the bigotry of memorial. For fidelity itself can become a banally conservative routine, preventing one from being astonished by the present. How not to distrust, anyway, that virtuous fidelity which betrayal accompanies like a shadow?" (3). In a later section of his memoir, titled "The Marrano Enigma," Bensaïd continues his critical reflection on the bigotry of memorial and political responsibility, referring to the "imaginary Marrano" as "an ambivalence, refractory to roots and rootings. An intimate wound" with "an aptitude to perform this game of hide and seek that escapes the identifications of police and tyranny" (284). He ends these reflections on "the marrano enigma" (no reference to Spirit here, either with or without quotation marks or capitalization, for they evoke very different gestures) with the following reference to the political: "And certainly there have been, and probably still will be, many Marrano communists. . . . The Marrano is both patient and impatient. Slowly. He bets on the long run" (284). The Marrano enigma for Bensaïd is the time, the duration, of survival extended in the absence of constancy, steadfastness, and the conservative demands of loyalty. In the marrano enigma there are no friends and no enemies. As Bensaïd puts it, the marrano enigma—which remains enigmatic on account of its distance from any spirit of familialism, brethren, kinship, identity, or difference—marks "an escape toward the excluded third option, an endurance to give life to a text beneath the text, and another still beneath the subtext" (284). In this sense, the marrano enigma for Bensaïd is exposure to language and never-ending reading, in a relation of incommensurable distance from the legal fiction of the social bond so often presupposed in the word "we."

I am struck (only figuratively, of course, though this does not mean we are not talking here, today, about a history and practice of violence) by the curious homework we have been invited to think together, individually and as a group, under the banner of—and therefore in the name of—a Marrano Spirit, on the way contributing to the determination of the spirit of this place, of this university, and in the heart of this institution that is dedicated explicitly, as are all universities, to the preservation of property; an institution whose subjective identity is the individuation of property itself administered in the name of *Bildung*. Does it mean anything to speak of a

Marrano Spirit, capitalized and without quotation marks, at the heart of the culture-ideology of individualized and therefore fully subjectivized property? Does it mean anything to speak at the beating heart of a university that is by definition alien to communal gift giving, and that announces itself on a daily basis in favor of the fully capitalized spirit of self-immunization, knowledge, and individualism? Of course it means something. It certainly means too much to address in these few pages. The very spirit of the corporate university—this propertied, fully capitalized subject—is to be found in its biopolitical labor of self-immunization against chance, in its management of security against an event, and therefore against the possibility of a political decision of any kind. In the corporatized university, the idea is that there can be no place for any decision and therefore no place for any notion or work of the political. No marrano enigma here, though certainly plenty of Spirit, and in particular that of Spirit (fully capitalized and without quotation marks)-become-institution, Spirit become will-to-knowledge, and, as such, Spirit become will-to-power; in the end, Spirit as subsumption and labor-extraction and therefore as the mark not of equality but of the work of dissymmetry and disproportion. This is what we are doing here. The biopolitical problematic of Spirit and of capitalization is everywhere, saturating all university proceedings at their origin and end (and perhaps not—or rather, surely not—only figuratively anymore). As Roberto Esposito reminded us in *Bios*, Nietzsche was always fully aware that "no politics exists other than that of bodies, conducted on bodies, through bodies" (84). Such is the Spirit of the political; territorialized, fully capitalized, and understood as biopolitical subsumption and collective instrumentalization as the fraternal subordination of language, and of life, to techne.

So what is the purpose of our "homework" carried out in relation to the question of the Spirit? What is its purpose? Or perhaps even its use-value? To what are we to give our language if not to the integrative, subsuming violence of a fully capitalized Spirit without any mark of doubling standing in, silently yet authoritatively, for the gathering and consistency of the familiar, perhaps even of the hearth itself? The Marrano enigma or register, with no mention of Spirit, can only be disloyal to, can only be the avoidance of, all homework, for it can only strive to circumvent all thought of the familiar, of the home, of the hearth, which is only ever a cover-up. The enigma can only be disloyal, expatriate, or unsuitable. Foreign to a final destination, it can only demonstrate hospitality to a step away from, rather than to full immersion in, the fully spirited fictions of metaphysical subjectivism that "unite us."

It is almost too easy to talk of Hispanism as the modern temporalization and spatialization of Latin-Romanic familiarity and confinement, or as the pious, metaphysical imperium of Spirit oriented toward the gathering of sameness, territory, tradition, law, and genealogy; toward the orientation of specific fraternizations grounded in the fabrication, iteration, and semblances of a common language: that is, in the constitution of a supposedly fully determined "We" (such as, "We, Here, Today"). Drawing on Reiner Schürmann's *Broken Hegemonies* (522), it could be said that the tradition of Hispanism that comes to us as our property, and that comes to us as homework in the name of Latin-Romanic reproduction (but perhaps less so in the name of thought) perpetuates "tragic denial": "Whoever seeks to think otherwise than in the service of a hegemony has nothing more to expect from the Greek vulgate that girds our epochal possibilities. The girdle is too tight; the encircling wall is impossible to jump. Whether overtly or covertly, the enclosure assigned to us continues to arrange everydayness in accordance with the morphology of the same and its inexhaustible ruses of subsumption" (522). "All that remains," continues Schürmann in this regard, "is to traverse that enclosure up to its boundaries and to trace the internal disturbances of its arrangements" (522). No supplementarity to be gleaned from any "*and* Hispanism" here, for Hispanism is our chosen and inexhaustible metaphysical ruse of enclosure and subsumption (that is, it is our choice for the limits imposed on us by representation). But this is not necessarily the same as saying that Hispanism no longer provides the conditions for reading, for, in full accordance with Schürmann, indeed, "all that remains is to traverse that enclosure up to its boundaries and to trace the internal disturbances of its arrangements." In other words, all that remains is to read responsibly with a view to the chance unleashing—to the leap—of the hegemonic fantasm.

To continue, then, all that remains is to read from within the enclosure of our chosen hearth, perhaps through a reading extended thanks to a certain underlying or clandestine relation to the history of tyranny, traversing and tracing the internal disturbances of the metaphysical spirit of subjectivism that underlies the violent intersections between nationalist and imperialist forms of anthropocentrism (be they called Capitalism, Hispanism, Nazism, Stalinism, or the University as the institutionalized, cultural and economic inflation of Spirit itself). What remains is not a Christian quest for the Spirit as that which lies beyond the measures and calculations of our given enclosure. Rather, it is responsibility to that which exists in a differential relation to the measures and calculations of enclosure itself. In this, I evoke and echo a particular sequence that I have opted to lift, somewhat gratuitously, without any particular fidelity in mind, from within the confines of the final novel of Roberto Bolaño's *2666*, namely, "The Part about Archimboldi." Working through this sequence will then allow me to reflect briefly on the relation between the marrano enigma and the thematization of responsibility that lies at the heart of, that shadows, Bolaño's major work.

Sweeping historical novel, bildungsroman, and simultaneously the emptying out of the narrative of self-cultivation, "The Part about Archimboldi" uncovers the story of the early life of Hans Reiter, Nazi soldier and future acclaimed, though invariably missing, novelist later known as Benno von Archimboldi, who came into the world in the wake of World War I and the disintegration of the territorial empire of Prussia. If the story of Archimboldi were to be placed in chronological order it would be the commencement of all the other stories contained in *2666*. But, as it stands, as both commencement and finality, it is the time and telos of progress exposed to the abyss. If it were placed in chronological order, as *2666*'s first novel, it would belong to the sphere of historicism as the anchor for a form of reason that transforms the experience of violence into the foundation of what would later be the known and the given. With "The Part about Archimboldi" positioned as the beginning of the novels comprising *2666*, "The Part about the Critics," "The Part about Amalfitano," "The Part about Fate," and "The Part about the Crimes" would all be different episodes in the quest to sublate and convert the violence contained in this novel into some form of dialectical reasoning with culture and the political, even in the case of the failure of the later novels to actually sublate and convert. *2666* would always be the name of a historicist melodrama handed over entirely to the successes and failures of the synthesizing operations of the dialectic. This rationalization of time would eliminate all chance from the novel by signaling "The Part about Archimboldi" always and only as the "no longer" that prescribes and determines the "not yet" that each of the other narratives generate in its wake. But as it stands, it is, as a "historical novel," nothing more than the opening up of a gap in the relation between the "no longer" and the "not yet," since in relation to its partner novels it provides for no genesis and no dialectical synthesis, even though it is the chronological story of the creation of Benno von Archimboldi. As such, it undermines historicist rationalization—it denies the bigotry of memorial that is guaranteed by the dialectical operation—since it simultaneously belongs to and does not belong to the category of "historical novel," for by the time we get to "The Part about Archimboldi" we have already seen where all the weight of these stories ends up, that is, in the closing lines of "The Part about the Crimes," where anonymous neighbors and outsiders perceive, in a world populated only by the silent cadavers of the slaughtered women of Santa Teresa, the uncanny sounds of laughter as the "only beacon that kept residents and strangers from getting lost" (633) ("no perderse"). With this in mind, "The Part about Archimboldi" belongs enigmatically to *2666* from within the register of its a-historicism, as do all its other parts, though this is obviously not the same as saying that *2666* is ahistorical. This internally dismantled historicism is the conceptual abyss that silently, secretly, traverses all the novels from "The Part about the Critics" all the way through to Lotte Reiter's desperate plea to her brother in the wake of the Santa Teresa murders in "The Part about Archimboldi": "'I don't know what to do anymore. . . . I don't have the strength. I don't understand anything and the little I do understand frightens me. Nothing makes sense. . . . Will you take care of it all? . . . Will you take care of it all?'" (890–91).

In this narrative world opened up to the historicism's abyss, the story of Reiter's life is placed in the frame of fascist and antifascist political and military (that is, imperial) conflict. In this story the young Reiter's father, crippled by the ravages of the Great War, laments the demise of the Prussian empire by assuring the future novelist, who throughout the first four novels remains little more than a silhouette or a shadow, that "the only people who aren't swine are the Prussians. But Prussia no longer exists. Where is Prussia? Do you see it?" (643). The sprit of imperial Prussia re-emerges, however, like a telluric Atlantis, as the family's collective Aryan gaze conjoins across the hearth of their home, while the adolescent Hans Reiter strives to avoid revealing the truth to his parents of how he passes his time: "When he got home, like a night diver, his mother asked him where he'd spent the day and the young Hans Reiter told her the first thing that came to mind, anything but the truth. Then his mother stared at him with her blue eye and the boy held her gaze with his two blue eyes, and from the corner near the hearth, the one-legged man watched them both with his two blue eyes and for three or four seconds the island of Prussia seemed to rise from the depths" (644). Conscripted into the German army, "in the service of the Reich" (679) as Reiter puts it, and therefore in the service of the destiny and spirit of his imperial homeland, Reiter becomes a uniformed wanderer as he moves incessantly across the European map of war, from Germany to Poland to France, from France to Count Dracula's Castle in Transylvania, to Crimea. On the outer margins of the German imperial homeland, on the border with its imperial counterpart the Soviet Union, the wandering soldier, who has lost the ability to speak due to an injury to his throat, finds himself in a village emptied of its inhabitants because a detachment "of the Einsatzgruppe C" had "proceeded to physically eliminate all the Jews in the village" (706). From within the heart of genocide, Reiter begins to look for a bandage to cover the wound in his throat. In his search for a dressing, the language-less Reiter stumbles by chance upon "the papers of Boris Abramovich and the hiding place behind the hearth" (707), located in a vacant farmhouse. Fascinated by the figure of the farmhouse's hearth as a camouflage—as a placeholder for a concealed, private writing and reading—Reiter, a soldier in the service of the Reich, "in the afternoons" would get "into the hiding place, armed only with Boris Ansky's papers and a candle, and he sat there until well into the night, until his joints were stiff and his limbs frozen, reading, reading" (708).

Immersed in the war and subjected fully to the mobilizations of interimperial combat, but in this hiding place momentarily not *of* the war, Hans Reiter reads the story of Boris Ambramovich Ansky, whose "parents were Jews, like almost all the villagers," who, at the age of fourteen, in a moment not of political commitment but of disaffiliation, is enlisted nevertheless into the ranks of the Red Army. After hearing the story of the death of a Jewish soldier who died fifty miles from Warsaw, Ansky "decided that he didn't want to be a soldier, but at that very same moment the officer handed him a paper and told him to sign. Now he was a soldier" (709). The story of Ansky intertwines with that of the formerly acclaimed, but consequently eclipsed and then executed Bolshevik science fiction writer, Efraim Ivanov. Ivanov had been a party member since 1902 and in 1910 is commissioned to write a short story about life in Russia in 1940. Titled "The Train through the Urals," this "cloyingly sentimental" tale is that of a Bolshevik utopia forged by industrialization and technological advancement as seen through the eyes of a child who is traveling to visit his grandfather who is a former Red Army soldier. On its publication, Ivanov is hailed as "a writer who believes in tomorrow . . . a writer who inspires faith in the future we're fighting for" (712). Ivanov takes Ansky under his wing, and Ansky too becomes a card-carrying Bolshevik. Under Stalin, Ivanov publishes his masterpiece, *Twilight*: "Its plot was very simple: a boy of fourteen abandons his family to join the ranks of the revolution. . . . In the midst of battle he's injured and his comrades leave him for dead. But before the vultures come to feed on the bodies, a spaceship drops onto the battlefield and takes him away, along with some of the mortally wounded soldiers. Then the spaceship enters the stratosphere and goes into orbit around Earth. All of the men's wounds are rapidly healed" (718). Again, the miracle of technological advancement and industrial modernity guarantee the resurrection and salvation of the Bolshevik revolutionary. Stalin reads the novel, but it strikes him as suspect (721). By the mid 1930s Ivanov has fallen out of grace, although no reasons are ever forthcoming as to why, perhaps indicating the incommensurable distance-proximity between banishment, murder, and the collectivist imperatives of the techno-communist state in its Stalinist form. In the first great purge of 1936 Ivanov is arrested and is convinced that it is the semblances of his science fiction—his metaphorization of the time of techno-scientific capitalism that he has forged in the spirit of communist revolution—that have sealed his fate. For Ivanov life comes to an end coldly, simply "shot in the back of the head and his body tossed on the bed of a truck" (728).

Reiter observes that Ansky's notebooks begin to lose their coherence as the Jewish Bolshevik recounts his desertion and return to his place of origin, the home and hearth where a young Nazi soldier is now reading in his hiding place which is not his, for it is now neither the place of the Jew nor of the non-Jew, but a crypt for the writing and reading that is the limit between one's murder and the other's survival. Reiter speculates that the hiding place in the hearth must have been constructed by Ansky's father, as a final paternal attempt to protect the son—to distance him definitively— from the prying eyes of the Bolshevik State's party officials. But the young German soldier also and immediately imagines the arrival of the Nazis— the end of all distance from the fascist state-form as everyday reality succumbs to military invasion—and the consequent annihilation of all the Jews in the village. In the aporetic space of the crypt-like hiding place in the hearth, in which the experience of the most intimate and the most distant, the limit between life and death, is rendered immeasurable, Reiter imagines Ansky's mother safeguarding the written word, "finding a safe place for her son's notebook and then, in his dreams, he watched her go off with the other Jews of Kostekino toward the waiting German punishment, toward us, toward death" (737).

Reiter is overcome by nightmares that reduce him to tears, but he remains nevertheless within the secret space in the Jewish family's farmhouse, "where he lit a fire and sat down by the hearth to reread Ansky's notebook. . . . He climbed carefully into the hiding place, which was warm, and he stayed there a long time, until the morning chill woke him" (738). One night he dreamed he was back in Crimea and that he had come upon a dead Red Army soldier lying facedown with a rifle in his hand. It is this recurring dream that finally brings him back to language, and that begins to thematize the question of responsibility that has haunted the novels of *2666* from the first page:

When he bent to turn him over and see his face, he feared, as he had so often feared, that the corpse would have Ansky's face. As he grasped the dead soldier by the jacket, he thought: I don't want to bear this weight, I don't, I don't, I want Ansky to live, I don't want him to die, I don't want to be the one who killed him, even unintentionally, accidentally, unawares. Then, with more relief than surprise, he discovered that the corpse had his own face, Reiter's face. When he woke from the dream that morning, his voice had returned. The first thing he said was "Thank God, it wasn't me." (738)

Reiter's dream voices his most intimate desire for innocence in the face of imperial force and techno-military annihilation. It announces the desire for a life lived at a distance from the historical responsibility of the German imperial state and its citizens: "I want Ansky to live, I don't want him to die, I don't want to be the one who killed him, even unintentionally, accidentally, unawares" (738). However, as a uniformed soldier of the German Reich there is absolutely no room for a clean conscience, for Reiter cannot not be responsible for the slaughter of the Jew since he is unintentionally, accidentally, and absolutely complicit in murder and genocide. But in the dream, Reiter's own death mask remains irreplaceable: "with more relief than surprise, he discovered that the corpse had his own face, Reiter's face." This safeguarding of a false innocence becomes the site from which responsibility in the face of the other's mortality is thematized in the dream, though its actual workings remain a mystery. What we do see, however, is the way in which an aporia of responsibility opens up in the immeasurable relation between the murdered Jew and the momentarily relieved and irreplaceable non-Jew, who by no fault of his own has already betrayed his ethical desire to remain innocent by the mere fact of living as a citizen in the service of the Reich. If Hans Reiter's dream momentarily uncovers a point of commencement for the question of responsibility—in which the German soldier and the fallen Jewish Bolshevik are conjoined in their relation to the bellicose time of technoscientific capitalism—the return to individual language and individual consciousness immunizes Reiter against the aporia of responsibility: "When he woke from the dream that morning, his voice had returned. The first thing he said was 'Thank God, it wasn't me'" (738). No longer dreaming, *It*—the corpse, the face, the Bolshevik, but also the corpse, the face, the Nazi— "wasn't *me*" he reassures himself. Reiter's return to language, it could be said, upholds a humanist immunization against the aporia of responsibility as he blocks off with his language of Christian consciousness—"Thank

God, it wasn't me"—the immeasurable in-difference underlying the relation between Jew and non-Jew. His return to language is a turn away from
the Jewish hiding place or crypt, and a return once again to the ideological
fantasy and epochality of the cogito; to the enclosures of the modern age
of techne, with no hiding place and no critique of semblance. In his willful self-delusion, he returns to the time of Spirit as the world-historical
destiny of the subject, which is also the world-historical destiny of fas-
cism. As such, he distances himself from all traces of in-difference and
reinscribes what Schürmann calls the enclosure that "continues to arrange
everydayness in accordance with the morphology of the same and its inexhaustible ruses of subsumption."

But the relation to the death of the other that is never entirely other does
not end there. Indeed, this secret, most intimate tale of ethical desire—"I
want Ansky to live, I don't want him to die, I don't want to be the one
who killed him, even unintentionally, accidentally, unawares" (738)—a tale
that cannot be told at a distance from ethical self-betrayal and self-sacrifice
since it is the story of a soldier already "in the service of the Reich" (679),
soon makes itself public though still hidden from view, as Reiter listens to
the sinister life story of Leo Sammer. Sammer is the living embodiment of
the banality of evil who tells Reiter the story of how he organized the murder of hundreds of Jews, eschewing responsibility while still safeguarding
a place for individual ethics by affirming that "anyone else in my place . . .
would have killed all those Jews with his own hands. I didn't. It isn't in my
nature" (767). Sammer is strangled to death, and Reiter is a suspect but
cannot be assigned guilt (767), though if he were in fact the murderer (and
the insinuation is that he is) then it could be said that he put Sammer to
death out of a sense of responsibility to the language of Ansky's notebooks
that led him to betray his own ethical desire for innocence, to embrace
fully the nonethical and the heretical—no longer "Thou shalt not kill" but
its opposite—and to do so in the name of a treacherous duty toward the
other that can never be distanced or separated from fidelity. His absolute
sense of responsibility would have led him inevitably, reasonably, down
the aporetic, practical, agential path of ethical self-sacrifice and betrayal.
There would be no other way to act responsibly.

It is in the wake of this aporetic path toward responsibility that Reiter becomes a writer, on the way betraying his inherited name and Prussian origin to the pseudonym Benno von Archimboldi (784) in an act of
renaming—of initiating the performance of a game of hide and seek in
order to escape, perhaps, his own historical bond with tyranny—that will

convert him into the silhouette or specter that he is throughout the other four novels that simultaneously precede and follow "The Part about Archimboldi." It is at this moment that Reiter becomes a haunting rendered from his origin by a kind of *becoming-marrano*, which we could understand as a becoming-minoritarian to the extent that he is withdrawn from his majoritarian markers of historical imperial domination—his living "in the service of the Reich"—through a transitive process initiated in the Jewish hiding place in the hearth, through his exposure to Ansky's notebooks on the frontier between fascist and soviet empires, while also passing through the aporias of his nightmare and the limitations of his ethical desire for innocence, passing also potentially through the murder of the bureaucratic murderer of Jews, Leo Sammer. My contention, then, is that it is through this withdrawal from, or deterritorialization of, the majoritarian, that Reiter's agency as a novelist initiates a bifurcation toward becoming-minoritarian.

Once again, the aporia of responsibility underlies the question of becoming-minoritarian in "The Part about Archimboldi," which I have also referred to here as Reiter's process of becoming-marrano. I think we can talk in these terms in reference to the silhouette-like figure of Archimboldi because the enigma of becoming-marrano applies as much to the nonmarrano as it does to the marrano, since the marrano enigma is not an identity but a refracting practice, a way of acting and surviving in the face of tyranny in such a way that murder and innocence are incommensurably conjoined as the most intimate wound of nonbelonging; of having no home or hearth, and of existing without familialism, brethren, kinship, identity, or difference, while always and only in the shadow of (in)justice.

Reiter's game of hide and seek designed to escape the identifications of police and tyranny begins when he approaches an old man in order to rent his French typewriter, with a view to completing and transcribing his first novel, *Lüdicke*:

> The man took an accounting book out of his desk and wanted to know his name. Reiter said the first thing that came into his head.
>
> "My name is Benno von Archimboldi."
>
> The old man looked him in the eye and said don't play games with me, what's your real name?
>
> "My name is Benno von Archimboldi, sir," said Reiter, "and if you think I'm joking I'd better go."
>
> For a few seconds both were silent. (784)

It is at this point that the old man addresses the perils of purity and will, limitless responsibility, and the pathetic underpinnings of exculpation while Reiter slowly becomes other-than-himself:

> "This country," he said to Reiter, who that afternoon, perhaps, became Archimboldi, "has tried to topple any number of countries into the abyss in the name of purity and will. As far as I'm concerned, you understand, purity and will are utter tripe. Thanks to purity and will we've all, every one of us, hear me you, become cowards and thugs, which in the end are one and the same. Now we sob and moan and say we didn't know! We had no idea! It was the Nazis! We never would have done such a thing! We know how to whimper. We know how to drum up sympathy. We don't care whether we're mocked so long as they pity us and forgive us. There'll be plenty of time for us to embark on a long holiday of forgetting. Do you understand me?"
>
> "I understand," said Archimboldi.
>
> "I was a writer," said the old man. (784)

After this there is no turning back. Under the guidance of the old man's words—words that acknowledge the bigotry and cowardice of Reiter's paternal inheritance (the paternal legacy of purity and will), yet defect from that inheritance while foreshadowing the incommensurability of generalized guilt in the wake of genocide—Reiter will never cease to become-marrano, or Archimboldi. He will become-the-other, or, rather, he will become the-other-than-himself that is the enigmatic nonposition of the marrano.

2666 refuses to relinquish the abyss opened up by its own internal marrano enigma, or becoming-minoritarian, that is Reiter in the wake of Ansky, who also goes by the name of Archimboldi. The literary critics in the first novel, "The Part about the Critics," read and work institutionally like the Christian humanist metaphysicians they are, since they assign Archimboldi a specific destiny as their own supernatural yet absent origin, and then strive to commune around the fantasy of the future revelation of that origin and struggle for the novelists' symbolic resurrection to presence and "actuality," all with a view to truly experiencing the plenitude of his fully resurgent spirit. But they are awful readers doomed to failure from the very beginning, for there can be no life, renaissance, or spirit of rebirth, capitalized or not, in the life or language of a writer who eschews the bigotry of memorial.

Daniel Bensaïd has referred to the marrano as "an ambivalence, refractory to roots and rootings. An intimate wound" with "an aptitude to perform this game of hide and seek that escapes the identifications of police and tyranny" (284). In *2666* the Jews of the village of Kostekino try, but fail, to hide in such a way as to escape the identifications (the purity and will) of police and tyranny. After their annihilation the Nazi soldier, this future novelist and specter, searches for a bandage to cover up his neck wound, occupying their cryptlike hiding place and, by chance, exposing himself to a Jewish tale of treacherous Bolshevism and Nazi tyranny. In the end the marrano enigma is not a reference to an identity or a group. It is the sign of a becoming-minoritarian, the aporetic weight of which is assumed by a responsible silhouette of a writer that traverses a collection of novels situated insistently in the wake of the Hegelian-Marxist conceptualization of the history of emancipation of the one universal class, and also in the wake of its antifascist politics in the twentieth century.

It is in the context of the dissociation from modern historicism—a metaphysics that sublates and orients violence in the name of specific forms of political rationalization and dialectical synthesis—that *2666* invites us to consider an *other* scene for the political, a turn or detour "toward the excluded third option, an endurance to give life to a text beneath the text, and another still beneath the subtext" (Bensaïd, *Impatient Life*, 284). This is the enigmatic and intimate wound that drives the community devoid of community, without a bond, Spirit, or specific origin to bind or synthesize it, and therefore without identity or difference, devoid of purity and of the inherent fascisms of the will. This community devoid of community is the marrano enigma that always remains to be read, for it always remains open to—moreover, it reopens incessantly—the question of the limits of any virtuous fidelity to community, to friends, and therefore to enemies. As such, it questions the underlying conditions of civility itself. And it does so without disdaining or ignoring the aporia of responsibility that any notion of civility requires and extends, but cannot ever contain, synthesize, or deconstruct.

WORKS CITED

Bensaïd, Daniel. *An Impatient Life: A Political Memoir*. Foreword by Tariq Ali. New York: Verso, 2013.

Bolaño, Roberto. *2666*. New York: Farrar, Straus and Giroux, 2008.

Esposito, Roberto. *Bios: Biopolitics and Philosophy*. Translated by Timothy Campbell. Minneapolis: University of Minnesota Press, 2008.

Schürmann, Reiner. *Broken Hegemonies*. Translated by Reginald Lilly. Bloomington: Indiana University Press, 2003.

CHAPTER 7

Infrapolitical Derrida:
The Ontic Determination of
Politics beyond Empiricism

Alberto Moreiras

> The spacing of time entails that alterity is undecidable. The
> other can be anything whatsoever or anyone whosoever. The
> relation to the other is thus the nonethical opening of ethics.
> This opening is violent because it entails that everything
> is exposed to what may corrupt and extinguish it.
>
> —MARTIN HÄGGLUND, *Radical Atheism: Derrida and the Time of Life*

The Step Back

In the "Fifth Study" of *The Idol and Distance* Jean-Luc Marion asks what
he calls a "brutal question": whether "distance," which in his book refers
primarily to the distance between the human and the divine, would come
to be "the ontological difference" (200). Marion wants to know whether
the very possibility of a new thinking of God and the divine must first
come to terms with the Heideggerian presentation of the difference between being and beings, since, from the early texts published by Martin
Heidegger, any possible abandonment of the ontotheological structura-
tion of thought (hence, also of the old thinking of God, the divine, and the
world) depends on it. Marion quotes *Identity and Difference* (1957) in order
to underline two terms in particular, namely, *Unter-Schied*, di-mension or
inter-cisssion, and *Austrag*, conciliation or resolution:

> If Being, in the sense of the uncovering Coming-over, and beings as
> such, in the sense of arrival that keeps itself concealed, realise them-
> selves as different, they do so by virtue of the Same, of the di-mension

[*Unter-Schied*]. The latter alone grants and holds apart the "between," in which the Coming-over and the Arrival are maintained in relation, separated one from the other and turned one toward the other. The difference of Being and beings, as di-mension [*Unter-Schied*] of the Coming-over and the Arrival, is the *uncovering and concealing Concilia-tion* [*entbergend-bergende Austrag*] of the one and the other. (Heidegger, quoted by Marion, 200–1)

We may neglect for the moment Marion's theological interests, which will take him toward an understanding of being beyond idolatry and representation but in the direction of "paternal distance." Our interest is to note that di-mension (or inter-cission) and conciliation (or resolution) are also political terms, terms with a certain political valence, or terms that can be read politically if we put them in a political context. We would be talking about a solvable excision, a tendentially conciliatory inter-cission, within a complex game that conceals and unconceals. It would perhaps not be too difficult to propose the transcodification into politics of *Unter-Schied* and *Austrag* in the Heideggerian sentences, but it is far more pressing to wonder whether the thought of ontological difference has already informed any political thought, any conceptualization of politics, over the last century, or whether the satisfied and by now rather willful forgetting of the ontological difference continues to inspire contemporary conceptuality.

Heidegger of course would have recommended a step back from such a forgetting, without which ontotheology would continue its not-so-secret reign in the unthought of contemporary thought: "The step back goes from the unthought—from the difference as such—towards what it is necessary to think. That is, towards the *forgetting* of the difference. The forgetting that it is necessary to think here is the veiling thought on the basis of *lethe* (occultation), a veiling of the difference as such, a veiling that for its part has, from the origin (*anfänglich*), withdrawn itself" (Heidegger quoted by Marion, 206). Heidegger never attempted to formulate any explicit thinking on politics commensurable with the difficulties of the step back, or at least not after the years of his own unforgettable political and moral catastrophe. But it is fair to say that Heidegger himself was not deaf to the political implications of a thematization of the ontological difference, which amounts to thinking the unthought in the tradition of Western metaphysics. Thinking the ontological difference had already a fundamental political incidence through the "technical" interpretation of contemporary politics it enabled. I will not spare you the rather long quote about a thought that is frequently glossed over:

The step needs a preparation that must be attempted here and now, taking into account being as such in its totality, how it is now and how it begins to show itself in an increasingly clear way. What now *is* finds itself marked by the mastery of the essence of modern technics, a mastery that is already manifest in all aspects of life through characteristics that receive various names, such as functionalization, perfection, automatization, bureaucratization, information. In the same way we call biology the representation of what is alive, the representation and formation of the being dominated by the essence of technics can be called technology. The expression can also serve to designate the metaphysics of the Atomic Age. The step back from metaphysics to the essence of metaphysics is, seen from the present and out of the image we have formed of it, the step that goes from technology and the technological description and interpretation of the epoch, to that essence of technics that remains yet to be thought. (*Identidad-Identität*, 114–17)[1]

Marion believes that contemporary thought must think the ontological difference not metaphysically. In the same way as Heidegger, who warns that the step back implies "a duration and a capacity of endurance whose measure we do not know" (*Identidad-Identität*, 114), or following him, Marion insists on the extreme difficulty: "These stakes appear as a task and a test for such thought only inasmuch as, precisely, the passage from the difference toward metaphysics and what it leaves unthought had nothing accidental about it, but came from an historial rigor whose constraints we barely measure" (Marion, *Idol and Distance*, 207). In his own critique regarding the early attempts of Jacques Derrida to deal with the step back through the notion of *différance*, through which Marion suggests that Derridean *différance* marginalizes ontological difference "in favor of an 'older' difference" (226) that "enframes it, situates it, and exceeds it" (232), Marion concludes that "Derrida's path . . . leads us further forward, certainly not in the way of an answer, but in the seriousness of the question" (232).

But Marion's critique takes place in the wake of a thought of the divine that Derrida would have kept at a (not necessarily paternal) distance. What remains to be thought is, then, whether politics could occupy, for Derrida or in the Derridean register, the place of the divine in Marion. This is a barely authorized question, since Derrida was never explicit in that respect to my knowledge. It would be possible to argue that Derrida never thought of himself primarily as a political thinker, and certainly not the early Derrida. But it is a question that could be rephrased as the question whether the task and the test of contemporary thought could be taken by Derrida to be, in the political terrain, those of attempting to think politically from a nonmetaphysical understanding of the ontological difference.

Marion refers, accurately enough, to the need for historical rigor. The possibility of a thinking of the political informed by the ontological difference is before anything else a historical possibility, since it can only be a possibility that is opened as such by history itself at the moment of its ontotheological caesura, at the moment of the step back conceived of as a relation with what has been covered over or forgotten by the historical tradition:

> Insofar as the step back determines the character of our dialogue with the history of Western thought, it leads in a certain way outside what has been thought in philosophy up until now. Thinking steps back from its business [*Sache*], being, and, with it, it takes what has been thought to a contrary position that allows us to contemplate the totality of that history . . . from the source of all thinking. In difference from Hegel, this is not an inherited problem, already formulated, but rather precisely what has never been asked by anybody alongside that history of thought. (*Identidad-Identität*, 113)

The difference from Hegel, of course, is absolutely crucial, to the extent that it sets the Hegelian thinking of the ontological difference in the realm of the difference between being and the being of beings, whereas the Heideggerian difference refers to something else, and quite otherwise.

Specters of Marx (1994) is the Derridean text in which there is a more decisive explicitation of his will to link something like a post-ontotheological political thought to a consideration of history and historicity as such. Speaking about then ongoing social transformations, Derrida affirms that they force us to think historicity otherwise: "This is where another thinking of historicity calls us beyond the metaphysical concepts of history and the end of history, whether it be derived from Hegel or from Marx" (*Specters*, 70). And he continues:

> In the same place, on the same limit, where history is finished, there where a certain determined concept of history comes to an end, precisely there the historicity of history begins, there finally it has the chance of heralding itself—of promising itself. There where man, a certain determined concept of man, of the *other man* and of man as *other* begins or has finally the chance of heralding itself—of promising itself. In an apparently inhuman or else a-human fashion. (*Specters*, 74)

On the same page Derrida refers to earlier attempts of his to accomplish a rupture with the metaphysical understanding of history in favor of a commitment to the Heideggerian thinking of historicity in the wake of the ontological difference. Deconstruction is here presented by Derrida, retrospectively, as always already political, and open from its inception to the promise that other sections of *Specters* will conceptualize as messianicity without messianism, that is, given over to an undetermined future that, however, keeps the possibility of emancipation and freedom. (But would that messianicity without messianism count as an effective recodification of the *Unter-Schied/Austrag* relation, if the messianic is the withdrawing excess that the ontological difference has always already inscribed in the ontic?) This new thinking of historicity was certainly already examined by Derrida as early as his 1964–65 Seminar at the École Normale Supérieure, recently published as *Heidegger: La question de l'être et l'histoire.*[2] In reference to those years he says:

> Permit me to recall very briefly that a certain deconstructive procedure, at least the one in which I thought I had to engage, consisted from the outset in putting into question the onto-theo- but also archeo-teleological concept of history—in Hegel, Marx, or even in the epochal thinking of Heidegger. Not in order to oppose it with an end of history or an anhistoricity, but, on the contrary, in order to show that this onto-theo-archeo-teleology locks up, neutralizes, and finally cancels historicity. It was then a matter of thinking another historicity—not a new history or still less a "new historicism," but another opening of event-ness as historicity that permitted one not to renounce, but on the contrary to open up access to an affirmative thinking of the messianic and emancipatory promise as promise: as *promise*, and not as onto-theological or teleo-eschatological program or design. Not only must one not renounce the emancipatory desire, it is necessary to insist on it more than ever, it seems, and insist on it, moreover, as the very indestructibility of the "it is necessary." This is the condition of a re-politicization, perhaps of another concept of the political. (74–75)

He could not have been clearer. A liberation of historicity, against its hijacking in the historical thought of Hegel, Marx, "even" Heidegger, is for Derrida a condition of re-politicization and the opening to a non-ontotheological concept of politics—something about which Derrida would have been thinking since, at least, the 1964–65 seminar on Heidegger (which includes, of course, substantial commentary on Hegel and historicity). These are also powerful textual motifs in the essay that Derrida would have written just some months before the beginning of that seminar, on Emmanuel Levinas's "Violence and Metaphysics," in which the fundamental theme of his *Auseinandersetzung* with Levinas can be picked up as a discussion of Heidegger's legacy and the best ways of going about it: historicity and violence, historicity and ontological difference, historicity and errancy or origin. It is therefore not out of line to believe that Derrida's explicitly political reflection, if one has ears to hear, must be referred to those years. But what is explicitly political, what is sufficiently explicit, and where and why is the line to be drawn, and who draws it?[3]

The Wise Men of Negev

My working hypothesis or proposal in what follows does not invoke, however, any explicit politicity in the work of the early Derrida. I do not need to do it, since I think politics is itself crisscrossed by historicity and is nothing but the concretion of historicity: Hence the essence of politics is not itself political, to parody Heidegger speaking about technology. I will call, more or less provisionally, the Derridean attempt to find an incipient articulation for his thinking of a new historicity to be revealed in the wake of the ontological difference infrapolitical: not a thinking directly on or of politics, rather the thinking of that which conditions politics, without which politics could not be thought. For me an infrapolitical perspective, which also seeks to understand the unthought of politics, would be the site from which to pursue initially the possibility of a new politicity, informed by the ontological difference, and by the attempt to think of it not metaphysically: to think of it, also, or indeed, politically.

My intention is, then, in order to offer a point of entry into Derridean infrapolitics, to raise some questions regarding Derrida's highly intricate reading of Emmanuel Levinas in his early essay on the latter, "Violence and Metaphysics. An Essay on the Thought of Emmanuel Levinas" (included in *Writing and Difference* [1967], but first published in 1964). If infrapolitics, as I have argued elsewhere, involves the double solicitation of the political by the ethical and of the ethical by the political, an infrapolitical perspective will only obtain if either politics or ethics, and particularly given their links to old notions of history that Derrida attempts to leave behind, are fundamentally altered in their notion. I agree with Martin Hägglund's critique of the alleged "ethical motivation" in deconstruction insofar as "the logic of deconstruction transforms the fundamental axioms that inform the discussion of ethics" (*Radical*, 76, 77). If a relationship to the other can be figured only from "the nonethical opening of ethics," and if "this opening is violent because it entails that everything is exposed to what may corrupt and extinguish it" (Hägglund, 88), then there is no nonviolent relationship with the other, and the fact of violence cannot be ethically regulated: It can only be ethically administered. This goes beyond destroying the alleged ethical motivation of deconstruction and leads into an understanding of the latter as ethically destructive. But then it would be equally fair to say that deconstruction can be defined as political only insofar as we allow the traditional concept of politics to waver as well. Political motivations must also be understood, in deconstruction, under the sign of destruction. Or else: Deconstruction is political only if the very concept of politics has mutated under its sign. An infrapolitical perspective—this is the risk of its definition—allows us to liberate the nonethical politicity deconstruction harbors as much as its impolitical ethics—both of which the critical tradition has somehow preferred to disavow, or at least to keep mostly silent about. I mean nonethical not in the sense of anti-ethical, in the same way that infrapolitics (or impolitics) does not refer to any anti-politicity. If there is a nonethical opening to ethics, and there is a nonpolitical opening to politics, then both ethics and politics, and infrapolitics in their double solicitation, must be placed in deconstruction.[4]

I start off in a double secondarization. The secondariness of ethics does not turn politics into originary and primary, the secondariness of politics does not make ethics primordial. There is also a nonpolitical opening of politics, an embedded and structural, desistent dissimulation of political irruption. For now I only want to anticipate that infrapolitics, if we can sustain it as an option, would be the region of theoretical practice that solicits the constitutive opacity of the ethicopolitical relation—hence admits, for every practical decision, of no preceding political or ethical light to mark the path. This, far from limiting it, turns infrapolitics into a kind of radical politicity that disavows every limit (without turning it exclusively into that). We could call it a politics of bad infinity, a shadow politics, and oppose it to any and all heliopolitics of the Good. (I have nothing against the Good, except that those who speak in its name tend to become scoundrels, in my limited experience.) Derrida would have sought, in a rather marrano way, from the very beginning of his itinerary as a thinker, an anti- or nonheliopolitical relationship to politics as a necessary step for the liberation of historicity from politics—that is, for the opening of politics to the ontico-ontological difference, or to the historical unthought of politicity itself. It is not then surprising that his attempt in "Violence and

Metaphysics" is to trace the residue of unthought heliocentrism in Levinas's work.

"Violence and Metaphysics" puts Levinas's work under an uncertain deconstruction. Levinas remained an important reference for Derrida, but perhaps in the sense that their moment of maximal proximity is at the same time, from Derrida's perspective, also their moment of maximal distance—there is an indifferentiation of proximity and nearness, which may also be the case, all in all, for Derrida's relationship to Heidegger. The 1964 essay sketches the figure of that double relation—proximity and distance—in its final pages on eschatology and empiricism.[5]

There is in Derrida's *Adieu to Levinas* (1997) a brief mention of a certain essay by Levinas on which Derrida chooses not to elaborate. In that reference Derrida hints at the fundamental notion of what I would like to call a Levinasian infrapolitics, which Derrida will always have preferred to deconstruct in order to reappropriate. Derrida refers to "Beyond the State in the State" ("Au-delà de l'état dans l'état")from *Nouvelles lectures talmudiques* (1996). Of it Derrida says: "Beyond-in: transcendence in immanence, beyond the political, but in the political" (Derrida, *Adieu*, 76). Let me do what Derrida does not do but obviously suggests and follow up on Levinas's essay. Levinas speaks in it of a certain hatred, not a hatred of democracy, rather a hatred of tyranny, of any and all tyranny: "The response of the ancients of Negev consists in refusing precisely tyranny, even amiable tyranny, and of reserving supreme popularity to the hatred of this irreducible tyranny and of the State that claims it" (Levinas, "Audelà," 63). And then he says that it is a hatred that is addressed

> to the friends of men in power, a hatred towards this friendship that is made of flattery and *delation*, site of all corruption. But a hatred that can be understood in a more profound manner, as a high degree of critique and control regarding a political power that remains unjustifiable in itself, but to which a human collectivity, through its multiplicity, and while waiting for something better, is pragmatically bound. (64)

The demos subjected to power is the figure of this hatred which accepts no hierarchy, no *arkhé*, except always in a provisional and revocable manner. Political power is for Levinas "unjustifiable but inevitable" (64). Its nonjustification is the very condition of democratic government, and the precise power, beyond the state, of the demos in the state: The nonjustification of power is, in other words, the very opening for demotic irruption in politics. For Levinas, "In this refusal of a politics of pure tyranny the lineaments of democracy are designed, that is, of a State open to the best, always on the alert, always to be renewed, always bound towards returning to the free persons that delegate to it, without separating themselves from, their liberty subjected to reason" (64).

There are at least three different sets of problems in the Levinasian fragments I have just quoted. First of all, we have the notion of a "beyond/ in," that is, a certain solicitation of the vexing inside/outside structure that we are asked to think not alternately, first in, then beyond, or first beyond, then in, but, if at all possible, simultaneously. Hatred is the term, or the affect, that allows for simultaneity. In the hatred of tyranny—as opposed to, for instance, the love of tyranny—we are simultaneously in and beyond the cause of tyranny, that is, in and beyond state power as such (hatred must have a ground and an object, but it comes from a site that seeks their cancellation, and it is therefore the trace of a beyond, which love, for instance, does not share). Second, hatred is explicitly registered as a hatred of complicity, of the chain of complicity or the chain in complicity that makes tyranny hegemonic through flattery and delation. This radically antihegemonic dimension of Levinasian hatred indicates a desire for a reconstitution of democracy always already on posthegemonic terms. And, third, the demotic hatred of complicity in tyranny has to do with a certain waiting: The sages of Negev are aware that the people only pragmatically accept, while hating, tyranny "while waiting for something better." Insofar as there is waiting, the text says, state power, and the power of the friends of the state, is inevitable: The inevitability is the very function of its pragmatic presence in the face of a certain enabling absence. But it is the absence whose cancellation the waiting awaits that makes tyrannical power also always at the same time unjustifiable, hence unjustified.

In his story of the sages of Negev Levinas gives us an account of political power always already subjected to its actual negation in the an-archic hatred of those who wait. But the negation is always at the same time merely latent in its irruptive potentiality—it can force an irruption of demotic power against tyranny, or it can also let tyranny be. Even in the latter case, however, the negating hatred persists. This is the "transcendence in immanence" of Derrida's commentary, which signals, I would say, his personal wager for a political position that would be "in politics, beyond politics." And in the State beyond the State. Politics is not simply the possibility or the action of transcending tyranny, and politics does not occur only within the inevitability of and resignation to tyranny. There is a simultaneity of anti-tyrannical political potency that affects both spaces insofar as there is a state always subjected to the possibility of demotic irruption (not tomorrow or in an undeterminable future, but always in every case) and a potency of irruption that cannot be conceptualized as already political as such. It is infrapolitical before the arrival of what must come, but not unconnected to it. The state always subject to the possibility of demotic irruption is therefore not, not quite, messianic democracy, but it is not, as undiluted tyranny, impervious to it either. An elaboration of this thematics through the Levinasian oeuvre would result, I believe, in the elucidation of a Levinasian infrapolitical perspective, that is, not just of his well-known suspension of the political in the name of ethics (in the secondarization of politics to ethics as first philosophy), but also, perhaps surprisingly, in the understanding of the necessary suspension of ethics in the name of a certain politicity that will have become no less fundamental, that is, no lesser aspect of first philosophy: the moment, always possible, when anti-tyrannical hatred ignores the inevitability of power. For that moment there is no previous light, either ethical or political—it happens, at the end of the wait and as end of the wait. If there is here a fundamental agreement between Levinas and Derrida (Derrida seems to admit that much in his 1977 essay), it is an agreement drawn on the disagreement indicated in the 1964 essay.

Secondary War

The word "politics" does not appear many times in Derrida's "Violence and Metaphysics," but it makes a crucial appearance toward the beginning of the essay, as part of a compound word. The word is "heliopolitics" (90). Derrida is discussing what Levinas calls "the break with Parmenides" ("Violence," 89), and a fundamental move toward "a thought of original difference" (90) and away from "the ancient clandestine friendship between light and power, the ancient complicity between theoretical objectivity and technico-political possession" (91). Within the economy of Derrida's essay, such ancient complicity, which refers to "the entire philosophical tradition, in its meaning and at bottom" as it makes "common cause with oppression and the totalitarianism of the same" (91), must be tested against the Levinasian presentation of the thought of Edmund Husserl and Martin Heidegger, with Hegel in the background. Derrida says on heliopolitics (while quoting Levinas): "In this heliopolitics 'the social ideal will be sought in an ideal of fusion . . . the subject . . . losing himself in a collective representation, in a common ideal. . . . It is the collectivity which says "us," and which, turned toward the intelligible sun, toward the truth, experience[s] the other at his side and not face to face with him'"

(90). Heliopolitics is therefore the name for an understanding of politics that would mark, in Emmanuel Biset's term, the "co-belonging of philosophy and politics" in the metaphysical tradition through a certain affirmation of a community of subjects, and which must now be vanquished and left behind (Biset, *Violencia, justicia y política*, 25).[6] Against heliopolitics the Levinasian term would be "ex-cendence" (Derrida, "Violence," 85), that is, "a departure from being and from the categories which describe it," following the Platonic notion of an *epekeina tes ousias*, a beyond the substance or Being which marks the Levinasian way of positing a radical departure from the philosophical and political tradition of the West and toward the conception of a "community of nonpresence, and therefore of nonphenomenality. Not a community without light, not a blindfolded synagogue, but a community anterior to Platonic light" ("Violence," 91).

As we know, it is the thought of the Other, the "radical priority" of the face of the Other, that organizes for Levinas the very possibility of ex-cendence, hence of a politics that could not be captured under the name of heliopolitics. This ex-cendence will be described by Derrida toward the end of the essay as "the *dream* of a purely *heterological* thought. . . . A *pure* thought of *pure* difference," whose "true name" is "empiricism," since "the experience of the other . . . is irreducible, and is therefore 'the experience par excellence'" (151–52). Through empiricism, says Derrida, Levinas "is resigned to betraying his own intentions in his philosophical discourse" (151) by opening it to nonphilosophy.

> Empiricism always has been determined by philosophy, from Plato to Husserl, as *nonphilosophy*: as the philosophical pretention to nonphilosophy, the inability to justify oneself, to come to one's own aid as speech. But this incapacitation, when resolutely assumed, contests the resolution and coherence of the logos (philosophy) at its root, instead of letting itself be questioned by the logos. Therefore, nothing can so profoundly *solicit* the Greek logos—philosophy—than this irruption of the totally-other; and nothing can to such an extent reawaken the logos to its origin as to its mortality, its other. (152)

The words just quoted mark at the same time the point of maximum proximity and the point of maximum distance between the Levinasian and the Derridean projects (and we can certainly read in this, a bit abysmally, a doubling of Levinasian community, or of the Derridean definition of it: "eros in which, within the proximity to the other, distance is integrally maintained; eros whose pathos is made simultaneously of this proximity and this duality" ["Violence," 90–91]). Throughout his essay Derrida has been at pains to show how Levinas fundamentally misreads both Husserlian phenomenology and Heideggerian ontology, how Levinas in fact presupposes both Husserl and Heidegger at the very same time he brings them into question. And yet, Derrida says, "the legitimacy of this putting into question does not seem to us any less radical" (133). We now see the reason: The step into nonphilosophy in the wake of a radical empiricism, the "irreducible experience" of the other, sanctions the legitimacy of Levinas's procedure, which nevertheless Derrida will not follow, or not all the way through. The question is, therefore, why. For me it is also the question about Derridean infrapolitics.

I think the answer might be attempted through the second mention of the word "politics" in the Derridean essay. Derrida is arguing that Levinas gets Heidegger's notion of being wrong, by conceptualizing it as a (part of a) philosophy of power, according to the following words: "To affirm the priority of *Being* over the *existent* is to decide the essence of philosophy; it is to subordinate the relation with *someone*, who is an existent (the ethical relation), to a relation with the *Being of the existent*, which, impersonal, permits the apprehension, the domination of the existent (a relationship of knowing), subordinates justice to freedom" (Levinas, quoted by Derrida, "Violence," 135). Derrida says that there can be, in Heidegger's work, no question of a subordination of any existent to Being, therefore no subordination of any ethical relation to any ontological relation, to the extent that "there can be an order of priority only between two determined things, two existents" ("Violence," 136). But Being, in Heidegger's determination, "is but the Being-of this existent, and does not exist outside it as a foreign power, or as a hostile or neutral impersonal element. The neutrality so often denounced by Levinas can only be the characteristic of an undetermined existent, or an anonymous ontic power, of a conceptual generality, or of a principle" ("Violence," 136); hence it is in no case a neutrality of Being. The second mention of "politics" comes, rather unexpectedly, a few pages later, but still in the context of this discussion:

> Being itself commands nothing or no one. As Being is not the lord of the existent, its priority (ontic metaphor) is not an *archia*. The best liberation from violence is a certain putting into question, which makes the search for an *archia* tremble. Only the thought of Being can do so, and not traditional "philosophy" or "metaphysics." The latter are therefore "politics" which can escape ethical violence only by economy: by battling violently against the violences of the *an-archy* whose possibility, in history, is still the accomplice of archism. (141)

The possibility of an-archy is still complicitous with archism. This potential reversal is similar to that which obtains between empiricism and metaphysics, or between nonphilosophy and philosophy. Or even between war and its opposite, hence between "politics," in the heliocentric sense Levinas condemns, and the "eschatology of messianic peace" that is the beyond of war in Levinas's *Totality and Infinity* (22). This is finally Derrida's objection, and it is not just any objection. It is, as I have already mentioned, the objection that separates both projects of thought at the moment of their maximum proximity.

The waiting position of the Negev wise men could not exclude a certain ambiguity. In the words of Levinas already quoted, "the human collectivity" is "pragmatically linked" to a political power "that remains unjustifiable in itself" "while it waits for something better." In the wait, which is a messianic awaiting, Levinasian infrapolitics finds its fullness and its limit. Derrida takes his distance on positing, even while not making it absolutely clear, an endless politicization without horizon, that is to say, in and through the very absence of that which one awaits. This is also an interruption of the waiting. He calls it "secondary war":

> This secondary war, as the avowal of violence, is the least possible violence, the only way to repress the worst violence, the violence of primitive and prelogical silence, of an unimaginable night which would not even be the opposite of nonviolence: nothingness, or pure non-sense. Thus discourse chooses itself violently in opposition to nothingness or pure non-sense, and, in philosophy, against nihilism. . . . This infinite passage through violence is what is called history. ("Violence," 130)

But why would one opt for the lesser violence as opposed to the greater violence? To a certain extent no reason is given. Lesser violence is an option for inscription, perhaps even a pragmatic one, a decision in the order of the immemorial, since no one will ever remember having made it: It belongs to the end of the wait and produces itself as the end of the wait, but it follows no previously given ethical or political light. It is, however, precisely and resolutely, the suspension of the wait, and it thus differs from Levinasian infrapolitics. It is a decision that takes place in the region of the nonpolitical opening of politics, it is the opening itself, and it is also in the region of the nonethical opening of ethics: against nothingness and pure non-sense, against nihilism. This is the obscure, infrapolitical site where it becomes possible to say that one would rather be in politics beyond politics, in ethics beyond ethics, or in history, without a beyond, in a history with no wait, beyond wait.

Since this is an important question for later developments in Derridean thought, and specifically for the issue of the messianic-emancipatory promise, let me dwell on it briefly. Martin Hägglund, repeating a Derridean motif already mentioned, speaks about "temporal alterity as the nonethical opening of ethics" (*Radical Atheism*, 97). For Hägglund temporal alterity is not a region but rather a constitutive condition of life that requires what Hägglund calls "originary discrimination" (98, see also 101). He goes on:

> Temporal alterity gives rise to both the desirable *and* the undesirable, to every chance *and* every menace. Hence, alterity cannot answer to someone or something that one ought to "respect" unconditionally. Rather, it precipitates affirmations *and* negations, confirmations *and* resistances, in relation to undecidable events that stem from the "same" infinite finitude. There is thus no opposition between undecidability and decisions in Derrida's thinking. On the contrary, it is the undecidable future that necessitates decisions. One is always forced to confront temporal alterity and engage in decisions that only can be made from time to time, in accordance with essentially corruptible calculations. (97)

Hägglund also says that "In [Derrida's] *Adieu* the nonethical opening of ethics is described as an arche-perjury or arche-betrayal that makes us doubly exposed to violence: 'exposed to undergo it but also to exercise it'" (99). But even all of that cannot answer the question as to why such originary discrimination must submit itself to choosing the lesser violence, even from a flexible definition of "lesser," which is obviously always a matter of interested comparison. (Lesser for whom? This reminds of a joke about Romans and slaves.) It would be easy to show that the greater violence could in a moment of decision posit itself as apotropaic, engaged in the name of a future diminishing of violence, but then the very notion of a lesser violence becomes moot or unhelpful. (A short story from Javier Marías brings the point home: The narrator complains to a friend that he has a business antagonist that is making his life impossible. The friend tells him he can solve the problem and sets an appointment for him with a fellow. The fellow turns out to be an assassin. The narrator is of course shocked and tells the assassin that he never thought the solution could be murder. The assassin tells the narrator he is sorry about the misunderstanding, but they must now conclude the meeting since he has another appointment. As the narrator exits the Palace Hotel, in one of whose coffee shops the conversation took place, he sees his business antagonist come in and approach the table of the assassin.)[7] One must conclude that, within "Violence and Metaphysics," Derrida gives no answer to the question, and the unanswered question takes Derrida, some years later, to his considerations on messianic justice, which in my opinion are equally nonresolutive. In any case, the option between lesser and greater violence, as a political option, would seem to remain secondary or derived, as it always refers to its conditions, to the region of the nonpolitical opening of politics.

The secondary war of history is the political scene. It is secondary in the face of a hypothetical originary violence, the founding violence of inscription as such, the founding violence of appearance. The co-belonging of philosophy and politics has everything to do with this "economy of war" (Derrida, "Violence," 148) that assures us there will be no end to conflict as such, there will be no peace but only the negotiated exchange between the inevitability and the unjustifiability of tyrannical power. So we are at a junction that can be conceived of, or that Derrida understands, as the crossing of two eschatologies: on the one hand, an epochal, polemological eschatology of erring; on the other hand, an eschatology of messianic peace. The first is associated with Heidegger, and linked to the years immediately following *Being and Time* (1927): "'Every epoch of world history is an epoch of erring.' . . . If Being is time and history, then erring and the epochal essence of Being are irreducible" ("Violence," 145). The messianic eschatology of peace, the awaiting and the attendant anticipatory move toward a time beyond politics, beyond violence, beyond division and conflict, a time of peace, is Levinasian eschatology. Alluding to right-Heideggerian positions, Derrida makes it clear in some brief remarks that it is simply not possible to ascribe an eschatology of the site to Heidegger, according to which conflict and division could also be finally reconciled through some return to the home. There is an erring through which Being dissimulates itself, veils itself through every possible ontic determination that occurs. The veiling of Being is history as such, within which "the sacred, it is true, appears. But the god remains distant" (Heidegger, quoted in "Violence," 146). The point is that the structure of dissimulation is a counterpoint to the erring that it institutes, which means that erring is precisely not all: and this minimal or maximal not-all is the Heideggerian eschatology. In Heidegger, in a certain Heidegger, it organizes history, as it were—it is history itself—and therefore also the opening and the possibility of a future time not subjected to principle or warranty. In Levinas, however, history finds its impassable limit in the anhistoricity of the ethical relation, which creates a beyond-history in the timeless time of the traumatic and immemorial encounter with the other.

Whether politics can be deemed to be unjustifiable but inevitable is, however, to be thought differently from the horizon of history as erring or from the horizon of the immemorial time beyond history. This difference is of course determining for any conception of political practice, but it also marks a different infrapolitical understanding. The ancients of Negev knew that there is a certain irreducible structure of waiting within politics whose tonality now doubles up. The minimal difference is also, opens up into, the maximum difference. This is the way Derrida describes it, in what to my mind is the fundamental point of "Violence and Metaphysics," which opens the very space of a nonheliopolitical infrapolitics that ultimately Levinas must abandon in favor of a peculiar Sun beyond Substance, his *epekeina tes ousías*, the Sun beyond the Sun of eschatological peace:

> [For Heidegger] Being is . . . the *first dissimulated*. . . . For Levinas, on the contrary, Being . . . is the *first dissimulating*, and the ontico-ontological difference thereby would neutralize difference, the infinite alterity of the totally-other. The ontico-ontological difference, moreover, would be conceivable only on the basis of the idea of the Infinite, or the unanticipatable irruption of the totally-other existent. For Levinas, as for Heidegger, language would be at once a coming forth and a holding back; enlightenment and obscurity; and for both, dissimulation would be a conceptual gesture. But for Levinas, the concept is on the plane of Being; for Heidegger it is on the plane of ontic determination. ("Violence," 149)

Derrida proposes an infrapolitics of radically ontic determination, clearly leaning on Heideggerian themes, every time and for the duration of time, that will not let itself be subject to any heliopolitical rescue, and against the Levinasian empirico-messianic infrapolitics—but also, at the same time, against any Husserlian-Heideggerian heliopolitics, and finally against Heideggerian heliopolitics, always latent or otherwise readable in the Heideggerian text. For the Levinas of the *Nouvelles lectures talmudiques*, as we saw, democratic politics occurs in the radical solicitation of tyrannical power, understood as unjustified but inevitable at and in the time of waiting. Demotic irruption can always happen in history, within history, that is, until the waiting is over and politics ceases altogether (or until an analogical claim is made that such is already the case, as it will have happened in every hegemonic political regime certain of itself). What I am calling Derridean infrapolitics suspends the waiting and posits an endless but in every case imminent political horizon marked both by erring and by the questioning of every dissimulation, where no analogical claims become possible because they are in advance consigned to unjustifiability. If there is, in that double perspective, a radical co-belonging of politics and thought in the shadow of heliopolitics, against all tyranny, and this time without a remainder, then it happens because the subtraction of politics, the difference of politics with itself—the Levinasian hatred of the complicitous friends of the tyrant equals the hatred of the tyrant—refers to its nonpolitical opening: to what sub-ceeds political errancy, which politics guards but also incessantly destroys.

Coda

I want to end with a brief gloss of what a Derridean option for an eschatology of erring or errancy may mean for infrapolitical reflection but I want to refrain from any attributions to Derrida of things he did not explicitly affirm. They could be implicit, whether in "Violence and Metaphysics" or elsewhere, but the reader will have to decide for himself or herself. In any case, what follows is no longer necessarily an interpretation of the Derridean 1964 essay, but rather aims at reading Heidegger's 1930 essay "On the Essence of Truth," the final version of which appeared in *Pathmarks* (1967, but the book was expanded and revised in 1976). Apologies for what will read as an abrupt and selective summary.[8]

In the Note added to the end of the text Heidegger says that in the phrase "the truth of essence" (from which the essence of truth must arise, after interpretation) it is important to understand "essence" verbally not nominally, and that such a change in understanding determines that in the phrase "remaining still within metaphysical presentation, Beyng is thought as the difference that holds sway between Being and beings" (153). "Truth" refers to a "sheltering that clears as the fundamental trait of Being" (153). But that truth of essence that still corresponds to metaphysical presentation mutates into "the essence of truth": "The answer to the question of the essence of truth is the saying of a turning within the history of Beyng. Because the sheltering that clears belongs to it, Beyng appears originarily in the light of concealing withdrawal. The name of this clearing is *aletheia*" (154).

The turning there named corresponds to "decisive steps" vis-à-vis *Being and Time*, through which we find access to a notion of truth as "ek-sistent freedom" and "as concealing and as errancy" (154). The concealing withdrawal as truth, or the truth as concealing withdrawal, implies a "change in the questioning that belongs to the overcoming of metaphysics" (170). Heidegger claims, therefore, that such a discovery is already the result, or performs in itself, a decisive movement in the recuperation of the ontological difference. "Beyng" (*Seyn*) is now errancy, and with it "every kind of anthropology and all subjectivity of the human being as subject is not merely left behind" (154). Rather, with it we proceed to a "transformed historical position" (154). Errancy is already, Heidegger says not only in 1930 but also through the period of publication and republication of *Pathmarks*, postmetaphysical thought, or a move toward it. Barely three years after *Being and Time* Heidegger takes a tenuous but clearly stated distance from all politics of Being and from the overwhelming metaphorization of Being as forgetfulness. In "On the Essence of Truth" there is talk of an opening in comportment, of a freedom, ek-sistent, proper to Dasein, that consists of relating to truth as letting-be of beings, in both the objective and subjective senses of the genitive. Letting-be must be actively understood, not in the fallen sense of leaving alone: It is a letting be of the thing, letting it be what it is, also as concealing withdrawal and as sheltering that clears. The proposed comportment has to do with a relation with the open region where things can be let be. That open region is truth as *aletheia*. But that also means that the historical human being can participate in the endeavor of distortion and dissimulation: "Because truth is in essence freedom, historical human beings can, in letting beings be, also *not* let beings be the beings that they are and as they are" (146). The mode of relation of the human being to truth moves toward being its relation to untruth. But untruth is not more proper to the human than truth—or less. Untruth also derives from truth as *aletheia*, as unconcealment, but in such a way that what comes into unconcealment is concealment, what is disclosed is closedness: "In the ek-sistent freedom of Da-sein a concealing of beings as a whole comes to pass. Here there *is* concealment" (148).

Concealment is untruth. Every unconcealment comes from concealment, hence untruth is "older even than letting-be itself" (148). Heidegger calls this "the mystery" (148: "The proper non-essence of truth is the mystery"). The mystery is the fact that concealment is the first thing that conceals itself, which means that truth happens first of all as untruth. "This bearing toward concealing conceals itself in letting a forgetfulness of the mystery take precedence and disappearing in such forgottenness" (149). In forgottenness the human being holds fast to what is at hand, what is accessible. "This persistence [in holding fast, the Spanish translation says: "aferrarse" (166)] has its unwitting support in that *bearing* by which Dasein not only ek-sists but also at the same time *in-sists*, i.e., holds fast [Spanish translation: "se pone terco y persiste" (166)] to what is offered by beings, as if they were open of and in themselves" (150). Heidegger calls the life where mystery as the forgotten essence of truth strongly abides "in-sistent ek-sistence" (150). In-sistent ek-sistence is the state of errancy. It is neither optional nor accidental. It belongs in an irreducible manner to the constitution of Dasein: "The errancy through which human beings stray is not something that, as it were, extends alongside them like a ditch into which they occasionally stumble; rather, errancy belongs to the inner constitution of the Da-sein into which historical human beings are admitted" (150).

If that is the case, what are the political consequences? Not, of course, that in political existence a catastrophic drift is always possible, and became actual for Heidegger. But it is conceivable that, from the postulates of "On the Essence of Truth," no Nazi politics of being would have been possible. Heidegger himself says in that text: "By leading them astray, errancy dominates human beings through and through. But, as leading astray, errancy at the same time contributes to a possibility that humans are capable of drawing up from their ek-sistence—the possibility that, by experiencing errancy itself and by not mistaking the mystery of Da-sein, they *not* let themselves be led astray" (151).

The latter is a political or an infrapolitical word—perhaps the clearest indication of a Heideggerian infrapolitics: to experience errancy itself as errancy, against every mythical projection, in the nakedness of a traumatic awakening: awakening to forgottenness as forgottenness. In errancy as errancy in-sistent ek-sistence unforgets the forgottenness of the mystery. An eschatology of errancy—which I tried to show earlier becomes Derrida's own wager—is the infrapolitical attempt at an impossible memory that it would be best not to call promise. Its name—Heidegger calls it "freedom" (151)—is the passage to the act of a demotic errancy that understands its main qualification—nothing else is necessary—is to know no one is qualified, because "nadie es más que nadie," nobody is subjected to anybody else's truth, and nobody is trivially a subject to truth.[9]

NOTES

1. I have translated from the German original and Spanish translation found in Leyte's edition of *Identität und Differenz*.

2. In "Violence and Historicity," which is a meditation on Derrida's "Violence and Metaphysics" (1964) carried over to a study of the 1964–65 seminar, Michael Naas notes that we are far from having understood the complexity of the early Derrida's relations with Heidegger's work, and that we will not be in a better position until many other seminars have been published: "Philosophy of History" and "Silence," from 1959–60, "The Present (Heidegger, Aristotle, Kant, Hegel, Bergson)," from 1960–61, "The World

in Heidegger," from 1961–62, and "Error and Errancy: Heidegger" and "History and Truth," from 1963–64.

3. Fredric Jameson's essay on *Specters of Marx* includes some elaboration on several of the problems of the reception of Derrida's most explicitly political thought in the hands of the guardians of political correctness. That Western Marxism continues to be singularly reluctant to abandon its own presuppositions is not a surprise, but Jameson puts his finger wrongly on the wound a couple of times: "Derrida's reserves about Marx, and even more strongly about the various Marxisms, all turn very specifically on this point, namely the illicit development of this or that Marxism, or even this or that argument, of Marx himself, in the direction of what he calls an ontology, that is to say, a form of the philosophical system (or of all metaphysics) specifically oriented around the conviction that it is some basic identity of being which can serve as a grounding or foundational reassurance for thought" ("Marx's Purloined Letter," 37). This type of irony, which consists in refusing in advance the critical charge coming from any non-Marxist presupposition, thus defamiliarizing it, which turns that critical charge into something at best whimsical, continues with Jameson's observations on the relation between Heidegger and Derrida (Derrida would have gotten under Heidegger's skirt in order to vindicate Heidegger's alleged grandiosity and then better and more effectively throw him to the winds as himself still trapped by metaphysics [28, 34]). But the most equivocal moment in Jameson's essay comes with his reading of Derrida's reading of the Heideggerian essay "The Anaximander Fragment." Jameson comes very close to a rightist reading of Heidegger but is aware that he cannot simply blame Derrida for taking that kind of reading upon himself. He then proceeds to reduce the project of rethinking historicity beyond Hegel as a mere mourning process that motivates the apparition of ghosts and specters, hence disavowing everything that is relevant and original and should be taken seriously by Jameson himself in Derrida's reading—but no, as it is just a bit too critical of the productionist ontotheology of Marxism that Jameson himself shares, not to give it up.

4. Derrida refers to the "nonethical opening of ethics" in *Grammatology*, 140. I thank Erin Graff Zivin for reminding me of this passage.

5. I will indirectly elicit a question on later Derridean texts, on their sustained emphasis on messianicity and the structure of the promise. But that will have to be left aside for future consideration, which I will try in the context of an extended review of Emmanuel Biset's *Violencia, justicia y política*.

6. Of course, Biset's point throughout his book is that there is the possibility of an alternative conceptualization of the belonging together of philosophy and politics that deconstruction enacts. On my part, I would use

alternative terms to talk about the co-belonging: thought and infrapolitics, as opposed to philosophy and politics.

7. See Javier Marías, "Un inmenso favor," in *Mala índole*, 325–35.

8. I should mention here, and refer the reader to, Peter Trawny's book *Freedom to Fail* (2014, English translation 2015), published after this essay was already written, in which the notion of errancy in Heidegger occupies center stage. For Trawny it is one of the ways in which he himself attempts to come to an understanding of the specifically Heideggerian antisemitism and racism. See also his *Heidegger et l'antisémitisme* (2014). See, most recently, Jean-Luc Nancy's *Banalité de Heidegger* (2015), which is a provocative and thought-provoking book written in a certain dialogue with Trawny's reflections.

9. In a conversation that took place before the writing of this essay Arturo Leyte comments on the notion of "experiencing errancy as errancy" as an exception to mythical projections: "I think it may well be, provided one does not lose sight of the fact that with it one can also fall into a mythical projection—precisely by raising errancy to the level of category (or error as foundation)—since there is no position that can find itself permanently free from falling into a mythical projection, a projection that infrapolitics should definitely steer clear of. After all, from Heidegger's perspective, even logic was mythically projected into the exceptional position that defines itself as 'the position that does not result from a mythical projection.' Heidegger never stopped denouncing, in the wake of Nietzsche, the concept as an expression of error, but then it is a matter of not letting that 'otherwise than concept' (and what would it be?) simply replace 'truth.' The issue is very complicated, and Heidegger's little essay is a permanent challenge."

WORKS CITED

Biset, Emmanuel. *Violencia, justicia y política: Una lectura de Jacques Derrida.* Villa María: Eduvim, 2012.

Derrida, Jacques. *Adieu a Levinas.* Translated by M. Naas and P.-A. Brault. Stanford: Stanford University Press, 1999.

———. *Heidegger: La question de l'etre et l'histoire: Cours de l'ENS-ULM 1964–1965.* Edited by Thomas Dutoit and Marguerite Derrida. Paris: Galilée, 2013.

———. *Of Grammatology.* Translated by Gayatri Chakravorty Spivak. Baltimore: Johns Hopkins University Press, 1974.

———. *Specters of Marx: The State of the Debt, the Work of Mourning, and the New International.* Translated by Peggy Kamuf. With an introduction by Bernd Magnus and Stephen Cullenberg. New York: Routledge, 1994.

———. "Violence and Metaphysics: An Essay on the Thought of Emmanuel Levinas." In *Writing and Difference*, translated by Alan Bass, 79–153. Chicago: University of Chicago Press, 1978.

Hägglund, Martin. *Radical Atheism: Derrida and the Time of Life*. Stanford: Stanford University Press, 2008.

Heidegger, Martin. "The Anaximander Fragment." In *Early Greek Thinking: The Dawn of Western Philosophy*, translated by David Farrell Krell and Frank A. Capuzzi, 13–58. San Francisco: Harper & Row, 1984.

———. "De la esencia de la verdad." In *Hitos*, translated by Helena Cortés and Arturo Leyte, 151–71. Madrid: Alianza Editorial, 2000.

———. *Identidad y diferencia: Identität und Differenz*. Edited by Arturo Leyte. Translated by Helena Cortés and Arturo Leyte. Barcelona: Anthropos, 1988.

Jameson, Fredric. "Marx's Purloined Letter." In *Ghostly Demarcations: A Symposium on Jacques Derrida's "Specters of Marx,"* 26–67. With an introduction by Michael Sprinker. New York: Verso, 1995.

Levinas, Emmanuel. "Au-delà de l'état dans l'état." In *Nouvelles lectures talmudiques*, 46–76. Paris: Minuit, 2005.

———. *Totality and Infinity: An Essay on Exteriority*. Translated by Alphonso Lingis. Pittsburgh: Duquesne University Press, 1969.

Marías, Javier. "Un inmenso favor." In *Mala índole: Cuentos aceptados y aceptables*, 325–35. Madrid: Alfaguara, 2012.

Marion, Jean-Luc. *The Idol and Distance: Five Studies*. Edited and translated by Thomas A. Carlson. New York: Fordham University Press, 2001.

Naas, Michael. "Violence and Historicity: Derrida's Early Reading of Heidegger." Unpublished typescript.

Nancy, Jean-Luc. *Banalité de Heidegger*. Paris: Galilée, 2015.

Trawny, Peter. *Freedom to Fail: Heidegger's Anarchy*. Translated by Ian Alexander Moore and Christopher Turner. Cambridge: Polity, 2015.

———. *Heidegger et l'antisémitisme: Sur les "Cahiers noirs."* Translated by Julia Christ and Jean-Claude Monod. Paris: Éditions du Seuil, 2014.

CHAPTER 8

Deconstruction and Its Precursors:
Levinas and Borges after Derrida

Erin Graff Zivin

> One always inherits from a secret—which says
> "read me, will you ever be able to do so?"
>
> —JACQUES DERRIDA, *Specters of Marx*

> I've always found it difficult to read Derrida.
>
> —EMIR RODRÍGUEZ MONEGAL, "Borges and Derrida: Apothecaries"

In the introduction to this volume, I emphasize the importance not only of identifying Derrida's effects on the fields of Hispanism and Latin Americanism, but also of attending to the marrano inflection in Derrida's work. These tasks are neither identical nor autonomous. Rather, each exposes blind spots and opens possible avenues of reflection in the other. In this chapter—the concluding chapter of *The Marrano Specter*—I want to consider two possible "precursors" of deconstruction, from two quite different traditions: Emmanuel Levinas and Jorge Luis Borges. In the first half of the essay I trace the concept of the illegible demand (for reading) in the thought of Levinas and Derrida, suggesting that the most significant consequences of Levinas's can begin to be traced only "after" Derrida. ("After" here meaning, in the wake of Levinas's response to Derrida's reading of his work: a double mediation.) Then, through a reading of Borges's short essay "Kafka y sus precursores [Kafka and His Precursors]," I argue that if literary and philosophical precursors can be determined retroactively and anachronically (Borges "after" Derrida), intempestive reading—reading after whatever is untimely in the work before it—might serve as the condition of possibility for indisciplinary, marrano thinking.

Marrano Ethics

As I detail in the introduction to *The Marrano Specter*, many scholars of deconstruction identify an ethicopolitical turn in Derrida's "late" work ("Racism's Last Word," *Altérités*, *Of Hospitality*, *Specters of Marx*, *The Politics of Friendship*, *Rogues*, *The Beast and the Sovereign*, *The Death Penalty* seminars, to give some examples). In his contribution to the present volume, Patrick Dove warns against dividing Derrida's work into late and early periods, a gesture made, he says, intentionally or unintentionally, in the interest of "saving" deconstruction from criticism in the wake of the de Man affair. Dove suggests that such a periodization eclipses the ethical consequences of Derrida's first books, and the concepts developed in them. Yet it is indisputable that although we may be able to identify ethical consequences of his early work, which more often address concepts related to language and form, ethical issues (as well as political concerns, although I do not discuss them here) are more frontally treated in seminars and books from the mid-1980s on. *Specters of Marx* strikes me as a particularly compelling example that might bridge what we think of as two distinct epochs (thus showing them to be related, not disparate at all). Specifically, I am interested in the by now overcited ethicopolitical injunction from *Specters* that appears as the epigraph to this chapter: "Read me, will you ever be able to do so?" This demand appears as unreadable while, paradoxically, acting as a demand for more reading. I call this the ethics of opacity, of the secret, a marrano ethics, and the reading called for a marrano reading practice: a mode of reading that pursues that which is untranslatable in a text, a reading that identifies the text's precursors, counterintuitively and anachronistically, in its future interpretations.

Where does this so-called ethical turn come from? Is it possible to identify Emmanuel Levinas as a precursor to Derrida's ethical concerns or even his thinking about politics? As a first step, I turn to Levinas's concept of the ethical injunction, the demand of the other over the same. Martin Hägglund has convincingly argued in *Radical Atheism* that Simon Critchley and others misguidedly establish a relation of equivalence between the concept of the ethical (and the related concepts of the trace, the other, and the infinite demand) in Levinas and Derrida—to produce what Critchley calls "an ethics of deconstruction." Hägglund is onto something important: It is a mistake to rush to forge Levinas into Derrida as we would metal into metal as Drucilla Cornell, Robert Bernasconi, and Critchley have done (Hägglund, *Radical Atheism*, 76). He recalls Cornell's characterization of deconstruction as "aspiration to a nonviolent relationship to the Other" in *The*

Philosophy of the Limit (62). Critchley, for his part, has become something of a sensation in the United States, especially following his appointment at the New School in 2008 (he is series moderator for the *New York Times* column "The Stone," and, in 2014, Edinburgh University Press issued the third edition of *The Ethics of Deconstruction: Derrida and Levinas*). Critchley is perhaps the most widely read of the three and has most significantly shaped the idea that deconstruction is somehow inherently ethical.

Hägglund's critique of Critchley centers on two principal issues: violence and temporality. He claims that Critchley is wrong to detect in Derrida's work a nonviolent ethical valence, to establish a conceptual parallel between ethics in Levinas and unconditional hospitality in Derrida: "The ethical is . . . a matter of responding to alterity by making decisions and calculations, whereas the unconditional is the non-ethical opening of ethics, namely, the exposure to an undecidable other that makes it necessary to decide and calculate in the first place" (Hägglund, "Non-Ethical," 301). This is, of course, a reference to Derrida's "The Violence of the Letter," in which he defines "arche-writing" as "the origin of morality as of immorality. The nonethical opening to ethics. A violent opening" (140). Hägglund's argument concerning the relation between unconditionality and the ethical, nonviolence and violence in Levinas and Derrida is convincing but less important to our reading than the question of temporality. Hägglund insists that we must distinguish between a Levinasian concept of time (in which ethical responsibility is antecedent, comes prior, to everything else) and the Derridean notion of untimeliness. He reminds us that Derrida's reading of Hamlet, "The time is out of joint; O cursed spite, / That ever I was born to set it right!" (1.5.211–12), downplays the more common interpretation of the lines—that Hamlet is complaining that he was born at an unjust time, or that it is unjust that he should have to bear the burden of the times—and proposes instead the concept of a time out of time with itself, an a-synchronic time.

But I am not sure that Hägglund's argument concerning temporality is right. Temporality seems to belong to a cluster of concepts that Levinas revisits in response to Derrida's critique of his earlier work (in "Violence and Metaphysics"), so that when we read *Otherwise Than Being* we are already reading Levinas-after-Derrida. Derrida's principal claim is that although Levinas, in *Totality and Infinity*, aims to move beyond being, ontology, he does so within the confines of metaphysical language ("VM," 102). We thus find in *Otherwise Than Being* that Levinas has undertaken a radical experimentation with language: We may recognize some of the key concepts of metaphysics, but they are rearranged, unsettled, through a proto- or para-deconstructive syntax. The concept of passivity would be one example: It does not appear to counter "activity," its ostensible opposite, but rather aims to evade this opposition altogether: "passivity more passive than all passivity" (*OTB*, 15).

Temporality in Levinas undergoes the same unsettling experimentation. What at first appears as a chronological relation—saying (*le dire*) as "antecedent to the verbal signs it conjugates, to the linguistic systems and the semantic glimmerings, a foreword preceding languages" (*OTB*, 5), a "pre-original language" (6), "the saying which signifies prior to essence, prior to identification" (45), "a *prior* signification proper to saying, which is neither ontological nor ontic" (46), "the very respiration of this skin *prior* to any intention" (49)—is explained to be other than a past moment, locatable on a linear continuum. Rather, Levinas is interested in an anarchical past, a past-before-the-past, "a diachrony refractory to all synchronization, a transcending diachrony . . . a past more ancient than every representable origin, a pre-original and anarchical *passed*" (9). We can claim that this is a not-yet deconstructive, or insufficiently deconstructive, gesture, but it seems to serve as a kind of opening to the Derridean "always already." This is not to say that Levinas and Derrida describe identical concepts of time; rather, we witness the beginnings of what will arguably acquire a more radical form in Derrida. I want to suggest that it becomes possible to read Levinas in this way only *after* having read Derrida. (This is not a strictly anachronistic reading since, as I have noted, we are already dealing with Levinas-after-Derrida.)

Of course, "prior" may not, or may not only, signify temporal precedence. If we say that "ethical responsibility is prior to everything else," we can mean prior in importance (the arrival of the other is a definitive moment for my ethical being; of all the moments that constitute me as an ethical being, it is the arrival of the other that is the most important, inasmuch as it alone is definitive: hence it has priority in respect to its importance, its definitiveness); prior in time (the other arrives, and then I make a decision); or prior in terms of logical structure (the arrival of the other is the necessary condition for there to be an ethical response: If the other arrives, then necessarily my response to the arrival of the other takes place in, even defines, the domain of the ethical). Hägglund perhaps confuses these senses of antecedence or priority: an axiological one (importance), a temporal one (succession of moments), and a logical one (for x to be the case, y has to obtain). But the sorts of metaphysics that Derrida is interested in dismantling (Levinas too, on this reading) depends on this confusion, is at core this confusion. ("Beyond," in Levinas, poses this same problem.) Levinas's experimentation with language addresses frontally the confusion of axiology, temporality, and logic in order to come up with a way of thinking otherwise. When I arrive, in the next section, at the notion of the precursor, I will reconsider these differing senses of priority or priorness, and suggest that a precursor text doesn't have to precede another chronologically, it can precede it logically or axiologically.

I may appear to be defending Critchley against Hägglund, when in fact I, too, want to avoid, even reject, the argument that deconstruction is somehow inherently ethical. My issue with Critchley is another—yet my critique would allow for the possibility that deconstruction is neither reducible to nor incompatible with a Levinasian ethics. In order to expose the differential compatibility of Levinas and Derrida (against both Critchley and Hägglund) I'd focus, instead, on Critchley's treatment of what he calls the "infinite demand." In his 2007 book *Infinitely Demanding: Ethics of Commitment, Politics of Resistance*, Critchley draws a parallel between the Danish theologian Knud Ejler Løgstrup's idea of the "unfulfillable demand" and Levinas's "demand of a *Faktum*" (or a "fact of the other") in order to argue in favor of a politics that is motivated, at its heart, by the ethical demand. For Løgstrup, an exemplary instance of an unfulfillable demand is the sermon on the mount, the injunction that Christ's followers be perfect "even as your Father which is in heaven" (Critchley, *Infinitely Demanding*, 52). The impossibility of properly responding to the demand intrigues Løgstrup for its radicality: We understand the demand; it is legible, transparent, but we can never succeed in fulfilling it because we are human; we are unlike God; we are imperfect.

Critchley then turns to Levinas's own concept of the ethical demand, which he understands as similarly unfulfillable (and asymmetrical). Critchley makes only one distinction between the two: In Levinas, the demand is unfulfillable because of its incomprehensibility, which corresponds to an opacity at the core of the subject: "The ethical relation to the other is not one of comprehension . . . the relation to the other lives on as an imprint in the subject to which it responds but which it cannot comprehend" (Critchley, *Infinitely Demanding*, 62). Yet there remains a sense, on Critchley's account, that the ethical demand exhibits a positive quality: It is a buried secret to which we would be able to respond properly—or properly translate into what Critchley calls a "politics of resistance"—if we could only decipher or unearth it. Whatever remains opaque about the demand is underemphasized or suppressed by Critchley in order to highlight the similarities between Løgstrup and Levinas (and, elsewhere, Badiou and Lacan). Critchley thus joins the legions of Levinasians and anti-Levinasians that see in his work an inescapably ontological quality, and Hägglund is right to take issue with Critchley's conflation of Levinas and Derrida.

But what do we lose in the attempt to divorce the work of Derrida from that of Levinas? If a "responsible" reading would aim to make salient the differences between the two thinkers—to demonstrate, as Hägglund has, the inherent, irreconcilable contradictions between the concepts of hospitality, violence, and temporality in Levinas and Derrida—wouldn't a responsible (deconstructive) critique also aim, irresponsibly, to read Levinas against the grain, to identify the seeds of concepts that will later appear in Derrida? In addition to the account of temporality that Levinas's syntactical experiments uneasily share with Derrida's discussion of untimeliness, I can cite the Derridean notion of "passive decision" as the decision "of the absolute other in me, the other as the absolute that decides on me in me" (*Politics of Friendship*, 68) as an echo of the Levinasian "command exercised by the other in me over me" (*OTB*, 141). What would it mean, conversely, to read Levinas retroactively, intempestively, from Derrida, to read ideas, still latent, that can't quite break out of the ontological lexicon of the Lithuanian French philosopher, but which nevertheless find an afterlife in the work of Derrida?

It is only by reading Levinas through or from Derrida that we can begin to conceive of an ethical demand *not* as that which cannot be fulfilled because it is impossible, godlike, or impenetrable, but rather *because* of its simultaneous call for and denial of interpretation. We know from *Specters of Marx* that "if the readability of a legacy were given, natural, transparent, univocal, if it did not call for and at the same time defy interpretation, we would never have anything to inherit from it" (18). Let us pretend, for a moment, that Derrida is *not* speaking of the specters of Hamlet's father, or of the specter of Marx, but the specter of Levinas: What would it mean to inherit from Levinas's ghost, to resist reaching consensus about what this legacy is? If the ethicopolitical, spectral demand, for Derrida, is aporetic in its simultaneous unreadability and demand to be read, if the demand does not communicate a positive content but rather guards a secret that exceeds the play of hiding and revelation, what kind of reading can we attempt today, what kind of anachronic, untimely readings are possible? How does one inherit from, respond to, the marrano specter?

Borges after Derrida

Let's consider the relation between Borges and Derrida, two thinkers whose work has traversed, both thematically and performatively, the dangerous, murky border between literature and philosophy, and whose readers see in them—not completely without justification—fertile ground for comparison. They are, we are told, intellectually alike, for better or worse, to the detriment or glory of one or the other. Before I begin, however, I want to alert you to two things and to anticipate my conclusion in the form of a suggestion. The comparison between Borges and Derrida is impossible; what's more, it's highly unoriginal: In the 1980s, the Latin American literary critics Roberto González Echevarría and Emir Rodríguez Monegal attempted to trace the textual and conceptual links between Borges and Derrida, and others have followed suit since then. What I'll be suggesting is that the notion of the precursor that each of them, Borges and Derrida, addresses, and which is used by critics to place Derrida and Borges in relation to each other, is tied to a range of undecidable questions that, because they are undecidable, make different forms of exteriority intrinsic to the work of Derrida and Borges. The demand made by this undecidable, intrinsic exteriority alerts Borges's and Derrida's readers to the constitutive unlikeness of an author to himself or herself, of a tradition to itself, of a discipline to itself. Coming to terms with this unlikeness is the task of Latin Americanism today, still.

Why should we read Borges and Derrida together? Why should we be interested in any of the concerns I've only begun to list—relations, grounds, comparisons, foundations, originality—when what we've learned from Borges and Derrida, in very different ways, is to be highly suspicious of claims to likeness, identity, foundations, origins? Can we read Borges as a precursor to Derrida, or to deconstruction more broadly, as some critics would have it? In what follows, I'll opt, instead, to dwell on the sites in which such inquisitions might fail, or fall short, by proposing other inquisitions, such as why the question of the precursor continues to haunt Latin Americanism.

I won't provide a comprehensive list of the studies comparing Borges and Derrida. Instead, I'll briefly consider González Echevarría's 1983 essay "BdeORridaGES (Borges y Derrida)" and Rodríguez Monegal's 1985 "Borges y Derrida: Boticarios," not as representative studies, but rather as readings that symptomatize a certain approach to literature, theory, and disciplinarity, as well as to the broader question of identity and ori-

gins in Latin American and Latin Americanist thought. I will then turn to
Borges's 1951 "Kafka y sus precursores" in order to "unread" or "misread"
Borges as a precursor to Derrida. I will argue that in drawing on the example of Zeno's paradox of motion, Borges postulates a theory of precursors as retroactively determined: untimely, *intempestivo*, at once early and
belated.

To relate Borges and Derrida, González Echevarría embarks on an
analysis of the three epigraphs of the third section of "Plato's Pharmacy,"
the first and last of which hail from Borges's work: the former from "La
esfera de Pascal" and the latter from "Tlön, Uqbar, Orbis Tertius," both
of which, the Yale professor would like us to know, were not easy to find.
Citation, then, serves as the point of departure for the establishment of a
textual relation between the two thinkers: "Given that Derrida has taught
us to take seriously exterior, 'preliminary' elements such as epigraphs,"
he tells us, "I will reflect briefly upon the possible meaning of these . . . in
order to make several indirect observations on the relation between Borges
and Derrida" (207, translation mine).

Already from the title, "BdeORridaGES (Borges y Derrida)," we have
a sense of what will follow. If at first glance the title appears to mimic the
play with words, roots, phonemes, and graphemes characteristic of at least
an early deconstructive tendency, it is followed by the parenthetical differentiation of the two writers in question, announced in caps and married
by the Spanish conjunction *y*. Although the graphic scrambling would, at
first glance, seem to upend any thought of essential identity or likeness, the
words or semiwords that jump out do a very different kind of work. If we
read from left to right, the first fully formed word in Spanish is *de*, evok-
ing a sense of belonging, of pertinence or property: either in the sense of
home, of national or local origins (*soy de California*) or of ownership (*este
libro es de mi amiga Paola*). If I allow my eyes to be captured, instead, by the
capital letters, they may be tricked into reading *orígenes*, again, signaling a
desire to identify origins, beginnings, roots. And indeed, that is what the
essay seems to do: Beyond the veneer of deconstruction (the essay turns
on the idea of the supplement; it scrambles letters; it imagines literary and
philosophical language as a tissue of citations), it reveals itself as most interested in establishing sources, influences, and origins: "Derrida ventures
to indicate . . . that Borges is one of his sources" (212).

In the 1985 essay "Borges y Derrida: Boticarios," González Echevarría's
then-colleague Emir Rodríguez Monegal takes up the question of the relation between the two by once again returning to "Plato's Pharmacy." The

opening lines of the essay imply that it might not be necessary to read Derrida since the Algerian French philosopher merely repeats what Borges had already accomplished years before. "I've always found it difficult to read Derrida," the Uruguayan critic begins, in a statement sure to please a reader allergic to philosophy and critical theory, "Not so much for the density of his thought and the heavy, redundant, and repetitive style in which it is developed" (yes, Derrida's a bad writer, he seems to tell us, but I'm an agile reader):

> but for an entirely circumstantial reason. Educated in Borges's thought from the age of fifteen, I must admit that many of Derrida's novelties struck me as being rather *tautological*. I could not understand why he took so long in arriving at the *same* luminous perspectives which Borges had opened up years earlier. His famed "deconstruction" impressed me for its technical precision and the infinite seduction of its textual sleights-of-hand, but it was all too *familiar* to me: I had *experienced* it in Borges *avant la lettre*. (128, my emphasis)

The argument is straightforward but has a number of consequences I'd like to outline here. First: We don't need Derrida, because we have Borges. This might lead to a second, implicit point: We don't need philosophy, critical theory, and so on, because we have literature. Third, deconstruction's origins are Latin American (echoing González Echevarría's point that Derrida places Borges, a "marginal" writer, into the "center" of European discourse). This reverses the center/periphery, original/copy formal relation pervasive in literary criticism at least until the Latin American avant-garde movements but does little to dismantle these oppositions (notice the reference to repetition, tautology, sameness, familiarity: Derrida as mere repetition of Borges). Beyond identifying a (Latin American) precursor of French (and later U.S.) deconstruction, beyond positing a rehierarchization of intellectual geopolitics, the essay affirms the same logic of identity, of origins and originality that we witness in González Echevarría's piece and which is at the heart of the most commonly accepted understandings of what a "precursor" is, what work it does.

We see, here, that although González Echevarría's and Rodríguez Monegal's canon-expanding projects may seem antithetical to the identitarian impulse beginning in 1980s Latin American literary studies, in fact they are two sides of the same coin: If the former emphasizes high culture over low, institutionality over marginality, both concern, first and foremost, the question of origins, and an overdetermined, underthought affiliation between identity and origins, even when these origins are to be read through a cosmopolitan lens.

But what do we mean when we talk about a precursor? What is it that we seek, that we desire, when we search for such a thing? In the 1951 essay "Kafka y sus precursores," first published in the newspaper *La nación* and later in *Otras inquisiciones*, Borges reflects on the question of influence by enumerating the works that anticipate—in theme, in tone, in spiritual affinity—the work of Franz Kafka in order to postulate an unorthodox theory of the relation between precursor and heir. Borges carries out his argument performatively rather than, or in addition to, constatively. As I hope to demonstrate, by thematizing the idea of the literary precursor, Borges proposes a method of reading that moves beyond our conventional notions of source and target, origin and heir, and alerts us to the untimely quality of inheritance and/as the demand for reading on which Derrida will reflect decades later.

"I once premeditated making a study of Kafka's precursors," the essay begins (199). The first verb, the first signifier of action—premeditate or *premeditar* in Spanish—appears as a kind of reverse performative: Borges's "I" premeditates, or claims that he premeditates, as a counterintuitive entry into a meditation on the impossibility of premeditation, what we will come to see as the performative delinking of subject and effect. The introductory paragraph, however, still insists—if we are to read it at face value—on the notion of authorial intention, not yet read as fiction, which can be understood in relation not only to the work of the essayist who "intends" to embark on a study of x or y but also to a causal relation between precursor and heir, one that is rooted in time (Borges's narrative subject explains that he will list Kafka's precursors in chronological order). The "pre-" of the *premeditación*, which here signals, retroactively, that which shall not or cannot come to pass, alludes as well to the "pre-" of *precursor* (from the Latin *prae*, beforehand, and *currere*, to run) so that even in this strange opening paragraph that would seem to propose a timely study of a chronological phenomenon, we begin to sense the untimely quality: of the study and of the precursor itself.

The first—the "original"—precursor to Kafka, Borges tells us, is Zeno, whose paradox of motion parallels the problem of *The Castle*:

> The first is Zeno's paradox against movement. A moving object at A (declares Aristotle) cannot reach point B, because it must first cover half the distance between the two points, and before that, half of the half, and before that, half of the half of the half, and so on to infinity;

the form of this illustrious problem is, exactly, that of *The Castle*, and the moving object and the arrow and Achilles are the first Kafkian characters in literature. (Borges, "Kafka and His Precursors," 199)

In his discussion of Zeno's paradox, Borges not only provides an example of a thematic link between Zeno and Kafka; he also allegorizes the very relation between precursor and heir and, subsequently, between text and reader. But what, precisely, is allegorized here? How are we to understand the relation between a moving object and its destination (or its origin)? Suppose we think of the relation between the moving object and its destination (or its origin) as a figure for the relation between precursor and heir (or vice versa). Let us imagine, Borges seems to suggest, the infinite length of time it would take for the moving object to reach its destination (or conversely, the infinitely small distance the moving object would have to cover in order to begin to move) as an unsuturable gap between the so-called original and target texts. Could this not also serve as an allegory for reading more broadly?

Imagining Borges's story this way tends to make him a precursor, not just of Derrida, but of Paul de Man as well. (A dramatic and uncontainable proliferation of precursors is one consequence of reading Borges with Derrida: The closer we get to establishing the influence of *a* precursor, the more precursors we seem to discover, and the more a single precursor seems to have come before other figures as well. This, too, is a version of Zeno's paradox.) We know from de Man that "allegories are always allegories of metaphor and, as such, they are always allegories of the impossibility of reading" (*Allegories of Reading*, 205). Such impossibility of reading, for de Man, has to do with the noncoincidence between allegory and its antecedent: "Allegory designates primarily a distance in relation to its own origin, and, renouncing the nostalgia and the desire to coincide, it establishes its language in the void of this temporal difference. In so doing, it prevents the self from an illusory identification with the non-self, which is now fully, though painfully, recognized as a non-self" (*Blindness and Insight*, 207). At the risk of echoing Rodríguez Monegal, hasn't that point already been made by Borges, if not constatively, then performatively? Isn't that precisely the problem that "Kafka y sus precursores" stages?

What, then, of the rapport between Borges and Derrida? When asked in an interview published in *Out of Nothing* in the blog "Outward from Nothingness" about Borges's influence on his work, the philosopher responds in the following way:

What would be my spontaneous attitude to Borges? It's a pensive one. I am reminded of an interview with Borges, during a visit to Harvard in 1968. His father had a theory of forgetting that lingered with him. "I think if I recall something," his father said, "for example, if today I look back on this morning, then I get an image of what I saw this morning. But if tonight, I'm thinking back on this morning, then what I'm really recalling is not the first image, but the first image in memory. So that every time I recall something, I'm not recalling it really, I'm recalling the last time I recalled it, I'm recalling my last memory of it. So that really, I have no memories whatever, I have no images whatever, about my childhood, my youth." My relationship with Borges works precisely in this fashion; I have no relationship with him whatever. The only relationship I have with him, his writings, is his ghost—the traces of Borges.

A closer look at this interview reveals a Borgesian influence, but not on Derrida himself: The interview was published in, and refers to, the year 2012, nearly a decade after the death of the so-called father of deconstruction.[1] The apocryphal quotation appears to hail not from Derrida, but from Derrida's ghost, bringing together two crucial aspects of the work of Borges and Derrida: forgeries and specters, suggesting that literary inheritances—inheritances from a precursor—are present only hauntologically.

The interview with Derrida's ghost, whether it knows it or not, is acting out an argument that is made philosophically in *Specters of Marx*, and which appears as the epigraph to this chapter, in which a ghost returns from the past to make a demand: "One always inherits from a secret—which says 'read me, will you ever be able to do so?'" (*SM*, 18). Such a demand is doubly impossible, because it hints at the unreadability of the text, and the aporetic duty to read it. Here we are faced with the challenge of interpreting the link between precursor and heir and, as such, we are heirs to the generations-old problem, in literary criticism, of establishing an impossible relation: a problem that takes on an added cultural and political dimension in Latin American literary studies. An infinitely difficult problem that enjoins us to infinite reading: But what kind of infinity, what kind of reading? Such an injunction teases out the ethicopolitical quality of reading: In our encounter with that which is unreadable in the text, in the other, we are called on to venture a guess, to make a decision (an interpretation) about something fundamentally undecidable. Here, the ever-receding and ever-proliferating precursor resembles the ever-receding text: Whether we understand the chasm between precursor and heir, text and reader to be infinitely vast or infinitely small does not seem to matter. Rather, we are faced with the dizzying possibility of infinite choice (interpretation) within a given limit, a curve approaching the asymptote it will never reach. The necessary decision that reading entails involves a kind of violence: perhaps the very violence on which disciplines and disciplinarity are formed, and which is never too far from ethics, however counterintuitive it may seem.

As a mode of conclusion, I want to turn to the final sentences of Borges's text, in which he makes the case for a kind of bidirectional relation between precursor and heir, one that complicates the chronological, causal relation announced in the opening lines of the essay. Browning's poem "Fears and Scruples," he argues, not only anticipates or foretells Kafka's work. Through Kafka's work, we can return to the poem and read that which we could not have read at the moment of its composition, that which Browning himself could not have anticipated. The uncanny bond between precursor and heir, then, comes about not only in our reading of Kafka through Browning but also in our untimely, anachronic return to Browning from Kafka. "The fact is that every writer *creates* his own precursors. His work modifies our conception of the past, as it will modify the future," Borges offers, contradicting the Borges of the opening paragraph, the Borges that "premeditated," the Borges that would proceed in chronological order, the "introduction-Borges" that anticipated—and would be canceled out by— "conclusion-Borges" (201)

It is this relation of unlikeness that Borges emphasizes in the final sentences of the essay: "The early Kafka of *Betrachtung* is less a precursor of the Kafka of somber myths and atrocious institutions than is Browning or Lord Dunsany" (201). Browning has more in common with late Kafka than early Kafka does. Or, to put it another way, Browning has more in common with Kafka than *Kafka* has with Kafka. It is here that Borges gives the fatal twist to the significance—the meaning but also the importance— of a precursor. The precursor, we can now see, is that aspect of exteriority that alerts us to the constitutive unlikeness of an author to himself or herself. Borges is not Borges, Kafka is not Kafka, Levinas is not Levinas, Derrida is not Derrida, the precursor arrives, belatedly, to tell us. And it is here that we can begin to imagine a rapport not only between Borges and Derrida, but between literature and philosophy as two disciplines that, as they approach one another, never arriving, expose the principle of nonidentity at the heart of each (literature is not literature, philosophy is not philosophy, and—we could add—deconstruction is not deconstruction,

Hispanism is not Hispanism). I suggested that the comparison between Borges and Derrida was impossible. It's now clear what that impossibility really means: not that we cannot compare them, but that the point of the comparison is its undecidability. But it is an undecidability at the core of our notion of an author or his or her work: We never know which Borges is writing, early Borges or late Borges; we never know which Derrida we're reading, Derrida haunted by Borges or Derrida haunted by not-Derrida, "early" Derrida, or "late" Derrida. Our search for precursors, then, insofar as it symptomatizes a desire for identity, for likeness, for origins, is doomed not to fail, but to succeed: There are always enough precursors, narrowly understood, to go around, always enough fathers to kill anxiously, following yet another Yale critic.

The strange principle of intempestive unlikeness anticipates (again, retroactively) the words of Levinas, who characterizes ethical experience as the experience of noncoincidence with oneself in the splintering of time: "This being torn up from oneself in the core of one's unity, this absolute noncoinciding, this diachrony of the instant, signifies in the form of one-penetrated-by-the-other" (*OTB*, 49).[2] When we rethink the idea of the precursor from and through Borges—as a moving object that never departs and never arrives, infinitely early, infinitely late—we find ourselves, writers and readers, torn up from ourselves, penetrated by the other. The discipline that we invent, our Hispanism, "signifies in the form of one-penetrated-by-the-other." To read Hispanism, or Latin Americanism, through and from Derrida is to embark on new, absolutely noncoinciding inquisitions, new interdisciplinary or *in*disciplinary inquiries that hold open the possibility of an outside, or of an outside within: the unknown that structures every event of reading.

NOTES

1. *Out of Nothing* also includes apocryphal interviews with Kierkegaard and Benjamin

2. I want to thank Ronald Mendoza-de Jesús for pointing me in the direction of this breathtaking passage from Levinas in a public lecture at the University of Southern California on February 3, 2016, "Time Fails: Reading Ethics in Two Poems of Borges."

WORKS CITED

Borges, Jorge Luis. 1962. "Kafka and His Precursors." Translated by James E. Irby. In *Labyrinths: Selected Stories and Other Writings*, edited by Donald A. Yates and James E. Irby, 199–201. New York: New Directions, 2007.

―――. "Kafka y sus precursores." 1951. In *Obras completas*, vol. 2: *1952–1972*, 88–90. Buenos Aires: Emecé, 1989.

Cornell, Drucilla. *The Philosophy of the Limit*. New York: Routledge, 1992.

Critchley, Simon. *Infinitely Demanding: Ethics of Commitment, Politics of Resistance*. 2007. London: Verso, 2012.

De Man, Paul. *Allegories of Reading: Figural Language in Rousseau, Nietzsche, Rilke, and Proust*. New Haven: Yale University Press, 1979.

―――. *Blindness and Insight: Essays in the Rhetoric of Contemporary Criticism*. 1971. 2nd ed. Minneapolis: University of Minnesota Press, 1983.

Derrida, Jacques. Interview with Jacques Derrida. *Out of Nothing*. http://out wardfromnothingness.com/interview-with-jacques-derrida.

―――. "Plato's Pharmacy." 1972. In *Dissemination*, translated by Barbara Johnson, 61–172. Chicago: University of Chicago Press, 1981.

―――. *The Politics of Friendship*. 1994. Translated by George Collins. London: Verso, 2005.

―――. *Specters of Marx: The State of Debt, the Work of Mourning, and the New International*. 1993. Translated by Peggy Kamuf. New York: Routledge, 1994.

―――. "The Violence of the Letter: From Lévi-Strauss to Rousseau." 1967. In *Of Grammatology*, translated by Gayatri Chakravorty Spivak, 101–40. Baltimore: Johns Hopkins University Press, 1997.

―――. "Violence and Metaphysics: An Essay on the Thought of Emmanuel Levinas." 1967. In *Writing and Difference*, translated by Alan Bass, 97–192. Chicago: University of Chicago Press, 1978.

González Echevarría, Roberto. "BdeORridaGES (BORGES Y DERRIDA)." In *Isla a su vuelo fugitivo: Ensayos críticos sobre literatura hispanoamericana*, 205–15. Madrid: José Porrúa Turanzas, 1983.

Hägglund, Martin. "The Non-Ethical Opening of Ethics: A Response to Derek Attridge." *Derrida Today* 3, no 2 (2010): 295–305.

―――. *Radical Atheism: Derrida and the Time of Life*. Stanford: Stanford University Press, 2008.

Levinas, Emmanuel. *Otherwise Than Being, or Beyond Essence*. 1974. Translated by Alphonso Lingis. Pittsburgh: Duquesne University Press, 1998.

―――. *Totality and Infinity: An Essay on Exteriority*. 1961. Translated by Alphonso Lingis. Pittsburgh: Duquesne University Press, 1969.

Rodríguez Monegal, Emir. "Borges and Derrida: Apothecaries." In *Borges and His Successors: The Borgesian Impact on Literature and the Arts*, edited by Edna Aizenberg, 128–54. Columbia: University of Missouri Press, 1990.

―――. "Borges y Derrida: Boticarios." *Maldoror* (Montevideo) 21 (1985): 123–32.

Afterword

Geoffrey Bennington

"Derrida and Hispanism" might at first have seemed an improbable sub-title. One might have thought that Derrida's references to Hispanic litera-ture and thought being so few (really just a few allusions to Borges in the '60s and '70s), that "Derrida and Hispanism" yoked together two entities in an encounter that, while perhaps not as improbable as that of an um-brella and a sewing machine on an operating table, was at least the encoun-ter of two entities almost totally external to one another. In this absence of any real direct engagement on Derrida's part with Hispanic writing, one might have expected the volume bearing the subtitle "Derrida and His-panism" to treat, in a spirit of historical inquiry, merely of the "impact" Derrida's work has in fact had on this particular field of academic study (among any number of possible others) and be of interest essentially, if not exclusively, to those working in that field, to "rank-and-file Hispa-nists," as one of the essays calls them. Or else, still within this "external-ist" hypothesis, we might have expected a volume identifying and bring-ing to Anglo-American attention the (often excellent) deconstructive work done in Spanish, perhaps by philosophers, whether in Madrid (with a fond memory here of Paco Vidarte), in Buenos Aires, in Santiago de Chile, or in Mexico City.

That this in fact turns out not to have been the shape and fate of this book certainly has something to do with the book's main title, *The Marrano Specter*, which (or so one might think on a superficial reading), already preempts that "externalist" reading of the subtitle by allowing Hispanism to stake a truly internal claim on Derrida. This would involve not only pointing out the essentially "Hispanic" nature of the marrano (as several contributors here do), and then claiming Derrida for Hispanism by pointing out the demonstrable importance of this word or concept in some of his work at least in the last decade or so of his life. One would then probably point out that this is not just any word or concept for Derrida, but a word or concept Derrida uses insistently to describe *himself*, Derrida himself, and this would mean that Derrida *as such*, would thus be in some sense essentially "Hispanized," probably via the long historical line of the Algerian Jews. And Derrida himself might then be taken to provide a fundamentally reassuring (if still quite enigmatic) figure for us to use in understanding his work in general: "those marranos with whom I have always secretly identified (don't tell anyone)," as he puts it in *Archive Fever*. And this might then seem to add weight to the arguments of those who have always striven to identify the Jew in Derrida (to the point of claiming improbably that *Glas* looks like the Talmud), and even to add an infinite weight, given that the logic of the marrano, as is indeed laid out in several of the essays in the volume, is such that it makes of the truest Jew the most secret Jew, and thus turns the inaccessible secret "itself" into an infallible mark of identification and belonging.

It is one of the great strengths of the volume that neither of these scenarios is quite what happens here, for as all the contributors know very well, it is part of the disconcerting logic of the marrano that the "internal" claim is no more sustainable (though obviously much more seductive) than the "external" claim. Just because of the logic of the secret that makes a marrano a marrano, no marrano really "is" a marrano in any exhaustively specifiable sense. "Marrano" enters into the nonfinite sequence of "nonsynonymous substitutions," becoming one of the "quasi-transcendentals" (alongside trace, writing, pharmakon, and the rest) that hold Derrida's work together in its somewhat gathered dispersion, but that entail that no one of those terms (not even "quasi-transcendental") could ever become the proper name for what Derrida is endlessly trying to write. "Marrano" is an only apparently proper name for something (but it can be no thing) that involves an essential moment of nonidentifiability. Marrano will, then, precisely not have been *the* name. Whence the *spectral*, the ghostly avoidance of the either/or, something not answerable to any ontology.

Which means that the essays gathered here themselves present an interestingly gathered dispersion where the spirit of the work repeatedly, sometimes brilliantly, works through many striking figures of this logic of identifiability in nonidentification, ranging from the marrano "himself," through the disciplinary structures of Hispanism "itself," to the broadest reaches of Derrida's thinking in its engagements with Lacan, Levinas, and Heidegger. Such a dispersion does not entail any lack of focus at all: The shape of Derrida's thinking (if I can put it like that), its quasi-fractal proliferation and self-similarity, requires us to imagine new academic topographies that no longer rely on the one- or two-dimensional spaces of the traditional disciplines. The *n*-dimensional (where *n* need not be an integer) space of deconstructive thought allows for both the largest theoretical gestures (there are several here) and the most minute specifics of textual detail given with as much scholarly rigor as anyone could wish. This volume, in which "Hispanism" is both delimited and exploded (as in an exploded diagram) is thereby exemplary for new work in the humanities, in an affirmation as jubilant as it is sober, the always indirect declaration of the secret itself.

ACKNOWLEDGMENTS

The essays collected in the present volume emerged from two meetings on the topic of Derrida and Hispanism: a seminar at the American Comparative Literature Association meeting in March 2014 in New York, and a colloquium held at the University of Southern California in April of the same year, both of which were co-organized with Samuel Steinberg. The meeting at the University of Southern California was generously funded by the USC Dornsife Del Amo Foundation, the USC Dornsife Office of the Dean, the Comparative Studies in Literature and Culture Doctoral Program, and the Departments of Spanish and Portuguese and Comparative Literature. I would like to acknowledge the invaluable participation of Jon Beasley-Murray, Marta Hernández-Salván, Kate Jenckes, Natalia Pérez, Cesar Pérez-Sánchez, Willy Thayer, Teresa Vilarós, and Sergio Villalobos in both of these meetings. While their papers could not be included in this volume (because of timing and other considerations), their intellectual generosity is present in these pages, spectrally. At the USC meeting, Julián Daniel Gutiérrez-Albilla's introduction to the screening of Safaa Fathy's film *D'ailleurs, Derrida* and a lively graduate student roundtable featuring Vincent Cervantes, Ali Kulez, Erin Mizrahi, Gerardo Muñoz, and Lacey Schauwecker contributed invaluably to the intergenerational vitality of the event. Safaa Fathy kindly agreed to allow for the use of the marvelous cover image, taken during the filming of *D'ailleurs, Derrida* in Toledo, Spain. In addition to co-sponsoring the colloquium, the USC Dornsife Office of the Dean also contributed to the publication of this book. Finally, I would like to thank Tom Lay at Fordham University Press for his sharp and critical eye, and for his support of *this* book, and for books in general.

GEOFFREY BENNINGTON is the Asa G. Candler Professor of Modern French Thought at Emory University and one of the foremost scholars of the work of Jacques Derrida. He is the author, editor, and translator of more than two dozen books and more than one hundred articles on deconstruction, critical theory, and continental philosophy. He is a member of the French editorial team preparing Jacques Derrida's seminars (about forty volumes) for publication (Editions Galilée) and general editor (with Peggy Kamuf) of the English translations of those seminars (University of Chicago Press).

PATRICK DOVE is a professor of Spanish at Indiana University. He is the author of *The Catastrophe of Modernity: Tragedy and the Nation in Latin American Literature* (Bucknell University Press, 2004). His second book, *Literature and "Interregnum": Globalization, War, and the Crisis of Sovereignty in Latin America*, was published by SUNY Press in 2016.

ERIN GRAFF ZIVIN is a professor of Spanish and Portuguese and comparative literature, and chair of the Department of Comparative Literature at the University of Southern California. She is the author of *The Wandering Signifier: Rhetoric of Jewishness in the Latin American Imaginary* (Duke University Press, 2008) and the editor of *The Ethics of Latin American Literary Criticism: Reading Otherwise* (Palgrave Macmillan, 2007). Her most recent book, *Figurative Inquisitions: Conversion, Torture, and Truth in the Luso-Hispanic Atlantic* (Northwestern University Press, 2014), was awarded the 2015 prize for best book by the Latin American Jewish Studies Association.

JAIME HANNEKEN is an associate professor in the Department of Spanish and Portuguese Studies at the University of Minnesota. Her research focuses on Latin American and Francophone postcolonial cultures. She is the author of *Imagining the Postcolonial: Discipline, Practice, and Poetics in Latin American and Francophone Discourse* (SUNY Press, 2015), and recent articles in *Cultural Critique*, *Contemporary French and Francophone Studies*, and *homo oeconomicus*.

PEGGY KAMUF is the Marion Frances Chevalier Professor of French and a professor of Italian and comparative literature, University of Southern California. She is the author, editor, and translator of eleven books, most of which engage with the work of Jacques Derrida. In addition, she is co-editor (with Geoffrey Bennington) of the series *The Seminars of Jacques Derrida* (University of Chicago Press) and a member of the editorial board of the *Oxford Literary Review*.

DAVID KELMAN is an associate professor of English and comparative literature at California State University, Fullerton. He is the author of *Counterfeit Politics: Secret Plots and Conspiracy Narratives in the Americas* (Bucknell University Press, 2012).

BRETT LEVINSON is a professor of comparative literature at Binghamton University. He is the author of *Market and Thought: Meditations on the Political and Biopolitical* (Fordham University Press, 2004), *The Ends of Literature: Post-transition and Neoliberalism in the Wake of the Boom* (Stanford University Press, 2002), and *Secondary Moderns: Mimesis, History, and Revolution in Lezama Lima's "American Expression"* (Bucknell University Press, 1996).

JACQUES LEZRA is a professor of Spanish at the University of California, Riverside. His most recent book is *Wild Materialism: The Ethic of Terror and the Modern Republic* (Fordham University Press, 2010; Spanish translation, 2012; Chinese translation, 2013). A book on Cervantes, *Contra los fueros de la muerte: El suceso cervantino*, a collection of articles and unpublished essays, as well as chapters from his first book, *Unspeakable Subjects: The Genealogy of the Event in Early Modern Europe* (Stanford University Press, 1997), was published in 2016 by La Cebra. Two books, *On the Nature of Marx's Things* and *This Untranslatability Which Is Not One*, are forthcoming in 2017. With Emily Apter and Michael Wood, he is the coeditor of *Dictionary of Untranslatables* (Princeton University Press, 2014), the English translation of *Vocabulaire européen des philosophies*. Lezra edits the Fordham University Press book series Idiom (with Paul North).

ALBERTO MOREIRAS is a professor of Hispanic studies at Texas A&M University, where he has had an appointment since 2010. He has published about one hundred and twenty essays, and his books include *Interpretación y diferencia* (1992), *Tercer espacio: Duelo y literatura en América Latina* (1999),

The Exhaustion of Difference: The Politics of Latin American Cultural Studies (2001), *Pensar en post/dictadura* (2001, coedited with Nelly Richard), *Línea de sombra: El no sujeto de lo político* (2007), and *Marranismo e inscripción, o el abandono de la conciencia desdichada* (2016). He has also published about ten edited monographic collections of essays in journals or multivolume works.

GARETH WILLIAMS is a professor of Romance languages and literatures at the University of Michigan. He is the author of *The Other Side of the Popular: Neoliberalism and Subalternity in Latin America* (Duke University Press, 2002), *The Mexican Exception: Sovereignty, Police, and Democracy* (Palgrave Macmillan, 2011), and numerous articles examining the relations among cultural history, literature, and political philosophy. He is also co-translator of Roberto Esposito's *The Origin of the Political: Hannah Arendt or Simone Weil?*, published in 2017 by Fordham University Press.

THE MARRANO SPECTER

The Marrano Specter

Derrida and Hispanism

Erin Graff Zivin

Editor

FORDHAM UNIVERSITY PRESS

New York 2018

Copyright © 2018 Fordham University Press

All rights reserved. No part of this publication may be reproduced, stored in a retrieval system, or transmitted in any form or by any means—electronic, mechanical, photocopy, recording, or any other—except for brief quotations in printed reviews, without the prior permission of the publisher.

Fordham University Press has no responsibility for the persistence or accuracy of URLs for external or third-party Internet websites referred to in this publication and does not guarantee that any content on such websites is, or will remain, accurate or appropriate.

Fordham University Press also publishes its books in a variety of electronic formats. Some content that appears in print may not be available in electronic books.

Visit us online at www.fordhampress.com.

Library of Congress Cataloging-in-Publication Data available online at https://catalog.loc.gov.

Printed and bound in Great Britain by Marston Book Services Limited, Oxfordshire

20 19 18   5 4 3 2 1
First edition

CONTENTS

8.   Deconstruction and Its Precursors: Levinas
     and Borges after Derrida

Afterword

Peggy Kamuf

Some of the most vibrant Hispanists working in the United States today are the authors of the essays in this volume, *The Marrano Specter: Derrida and Hispanism*, which emerged from the 2014 conference on the topic. The essayists agreed to reflect on the figure of the marrano as a way into questions about their field from the angles of the sort of "theory" Hispanism has long reproved and resisted, for the marrano also plays a significant role in the late work of Jacques Derrida, recurring there with some frequency. By pairing the field's name with Derrida's, the title of the present volume opens the space of an encounter into which the essays collected here advance at their different rhythms.

The marrano, as traced by Derrida over the last dozen years of his life's work, is taken on there at multiple levels, beginning perhaps with the level of personal identification out of which unfold various figures of universalization. The identification arises out of the childhood experience among the Jews of Algiers who called circumcision "baptism" and Bar Mitzvah "communion," through a strange kind of assimilation to or compromise with the dominant Christian culture in which Judaism survives in remnants. In *Circumfession* (1991), Derrida confesses or feigns to confess: "I am a sort of marrano of French Catholic culture . . . one of those marranos who no longer say they are Jews even in the secret of their own hearts, not so as to be authenticated as marranos on both sides of the public frontier, but because they doubt everything, never go to confession or give up enlightenment" (170–71).

But from there the figure of the marrano is carried by a force of universalization to which Derrida gives explicit voice. In *Aporias* (1992) marrano comes to name the universal condition of an impossible relation to death as to a secret. "Let us figuratively call marrano anyone who remains faithful to a secret that he has not chosen, in the very place where he lives, in the home of the inhabitant or of the occupant, in the home of the first or of the second *arrivant*, in the very place where he sojourns without saying no but without identifying himself as belonging to" (81). Elsewhere, in "Abraham, the Other" (2003), Derrida patiently works out this transposition of singular experience into universal description. At one point, addressing himself in the figure of the marrano, he reads off its paradoxical law: "The less you show yourself as jewish, the more and better jew you will be. The more radically you break with a certain dogmatism of the place and the bond (communal, national, religious, of the state), the more you will be faithful to the hyperbolic, excessive demand, to the *hubris*, perhaps, of a universal and disproportionate responsibility toward the singularity of every other" (13). The marrano axiomatic of more-than equals less-than or other-than is associated by Derrida with his mistrust of frontiers and oppositional distinctions, impelling him, as he writes, "to elaborate a deconstruction as well as an ethics of decision or of responsibility exposed to the endurance of the undecidable" (17). Marrano thus names a hyperbolic, universal responsibility, a fidelity that breaks with every community, a secret destiny that sojourns without belonging, a dissociation that inhabits the social bond.

This latter essay, "Abraham, the Other," is in part a reading of a Kafka parable titled simply "Abraham." There Kafka repeatedly invokes "another Abraham," "other Abrahams," for example, one who could not get away from the house however much he was willing to answer the call to sacrifice. Or "take another Abraham," says Kafka, who likewise was ready to do the right thing, but he cannot believe that he was the Abraham addressed by the call. He fears being foolish and that "the world would laugh itself to death at the sight of him." Just imagine if the worst student in the class thinks his name has been called to receive a prize meant for the best student: "He came forward from his dirty desk in the last row because he had made a mistake of hearing and the whole class burst out laughing." In the midst of all these misprisions and malentendus, this other Abraham at one point fears that, if he answers the call, he will turn into someone else, and not just anyone else: "He is afraid that after starting out as Abraham with his son he would change on the way into Don Quixote."

Don Quixote? Even though, in his selective reading of the parable, Derrida does not wonder about this allusion to one of the foundational works of Hispanism, others now come forward here to pursue the reflection in the shadow of Cervantes, but also of Bolaño, Borges, Cortázar. It is a reflection on marranismo as it arises out of the language that first lent cover in that name to the refractory subjects who all the same respond, "Yes, here I am," like the other Abraham. Marrano was meant to have the force of insult, injury, *injure* in French, at once insult and injury. It was meant to be a wounding word. Swine. Dirty. Outcast. But at the same time marrano deflects, absorbs, or shelters in secret the other name. It keeps the one who keeps the secret. One is "entrusted for safekeeping, entrusted to a silence that keeps and guards so long as one keeps and guards it" ("Abraham, the Other," 6).

About a quarter century ago, in 1992, was the five-hundredth anniversary of the expulsion of the Jews from Spain. It was also, of course, the anniversary of the year Columbus gave the Old World a foothold in the New and took a first step toward the vast Spanish empire to come in the Americas. And in the same year, with the fall of Granada, Arabs were driven out of a newly unified and uniformly Catholic Spain. *Annus mirabilis, annus horribilis.* If we call Hispanists those who inherit and respond to this immense legacy in trust for the rest of us, then this volume is testimony to a trust well placed.

Los Angeles
January 2016

WORKS CITED

Jacques Derrida, "Abraham, the Other." 2003. In *Judeities: Questions for Jacques Derrida*, edited by Bettina Bergo, Joseph Cohen, and Raphael Zagury-Orly, 1–35. New York: Fordham University Press, 2007.

———. *Aporias.* 1992. Stanford: Stanford University Press, 1993.

———. *Circumfession.* 1991. In *Jacques Derrida*, translated by Geoffrey Bennington, 3–315. Chicago: University of Chicago Press, 1993.